Stop Writing New Books!

How to Find and Profit from Books Already Written and Available on the Public Domain

Gerry Marrs

Gerry Marrs Publications

Contents

Introduction

I magine this for a moment. You're wandering through a dusty old attic, the kind of place filled with forgotten keepsakes, creaky floorboards, and the scent of aged wood. Tucked away in the dim corner, hidden beneath years of neglect, sits an unassuming treasure chest. Though it's covered in cobwebs and surrounded by a halo of mystery, its presence is magnetic. You crack it open, half expecting to find a dull pile of old junk—but instead, a breathtaking sight stuns you. Inside are untold riches—not emeralds or gold doubloons, but something far more valuable in the modern world. Ideas. Stories. Images. Knowledge. All free for the taking. That treasure chest, brimming with infinite possibility, is the public domain.

Now pause and consider just how incredible this is. These aren't just any stories or ideas; they include the works of literary icons, historical narratives that shaped the world, illustrations that once adorned books and posters, and timeless pieces of music that stirred hearts across generations. And yet, for reasons that baffle the imagination, so much of this treasure remains untouched, unclaimed, and unknown. Millions walk past it every day, unaware of its power. But not you. You're here, standing at the edge of an extraordinary opportunity. All you need is the key to unlock its full potential.

The public domain is more than a dusty collection of forgotten works. It's a fertile world of creativity that belongs to you, me, and anyone daring enough to explore it. Imagine standing in an open field, the soil rich and ready to nurture whatever you decide to plant. That's the public domain. It offers the foundation, the raw material, for you to create something truly remarkable. Whether you draw inspiration from a 19th-century novel, transform vintage artwork into modern designs, or reinterpret the words of history for new audiences, the possibilities are endless. All you need is a vision, and this vast treasure is yours to use freely.

To grasp the immense power of this opportunity, think about some of the most beloved and iconic stories throughout history. Sir Arthur Conan Doyle's *Sherlock Holmes*, a public domain character, has been reimagined into blockbuster movies, acclaimed TV shows, and endless adaptations that continue to thrill audiences worldwide. L. Frank Baum's *The Wizard of Oz* evolved into one of the most famous cultural landmarks of all time, spawning adaptations across musicals, films, fashion, and beyond. Even Disney's unstoppable empire owes some of its success to public domain tales, like the timeless story of *Snow White*. All of these started as treasure in that proverbial chest, waiting for someone with vision to breathe new life into them.

And here's the kicker. You don't have to be a Hollywood producer, tech-savvy entrepreneur, or intellectual property expert to access this treasure. The beauty of the public domain is just how accessible it is. No gatekeepers, no hefty licensing fees, and no complex contracts standing in your way. The stories, poems, music, artwork, and even scientific works of countless generations are sitting right there, available for anyone who chooses to claim them. For you, this means an incredible wealth of raw material just waiting to be transformed into something fresh, relevant, and profitable.

Picture again the thrill of opening that chest. The excitement of uncovering a forgotten classic waiting to see the light of day again, or stumbling upon an idea that sparks your imagination in a way nothing else has. The possibilities are endless. Maybe you convert a dusty old novel into a modern audiobook. Maybe you take a collection of historical illustrations and turn them into high-quality art prints for enthusiasts. Or maybe you transform a 19th-century series of essays into a stunningly designed coffee table book. The treasure isn't just what you find inside the chest; it's what you can create from it.

You're not just exploring the past with this opportunity. You're connecting it to the present in new, creative ways. You're delivering something meaningful to today's world while preserving and celebrating the legacies of those who came before us. And on top of it all? You're potentially building a thriving business that generates income and gives you creative fulfillment.

By the time you finish this book, you'll know how to identify the most valuable gems hidden in the public domain, how to refine them into something new, and how to share them with an audience eager for fresh content. This isn't just a once-in-a-lifetime opportunity waiting for someone else to seize. It's here, it's now, and it's yours.

The public domain is your treasure chest. What you do with it can be nothing short of extraordinary. All you have to do is take that first step. The spark of discovery is waiting, and so is the chance to leave your creative mark on the world. Are you ready? Open the chest. What comes next could change everything.

Why Profit from the Public Domain?

You might be wondering, "Why is this opportunity for me? Why should I care about the public domain when there are so many ways to make money these days?" The answer is deceptively simple. The world is hungry for content. Stories, entertainment, learning tools, and fresh perspectives are more in demand now than ever before. But creating those from scratch can be time-consuming, expensive, and fraught with uncertainty.

That's where the public domain steps in like an unsung hero. The hard work of storytelling, researching, and writing has already been done by brilliant minds of the past. Your role is to breathe new life into these works, to make them resonate with modern audiences. And because the public domain is free of copyright restrictions, you have the freedom to adapt, revise, and repurpose these works however you please.

Now consider this. Every platform that connects creators to consumers—from Amazon to Etsy, YouTube to online courses—is growing exponentially. These modern tools make it easier than ever to turn creative projects into profitable ventures. Whether you want to create a stunning new illustrated edition of a classic novel, record an audiobook in your voice, or build a series of educational workbooks based on timeless texts, the opportunities are limitless.

The Journey You're About to Take

This book is designed to act as your guide on this exciting creative and entrepreneurial journey. Throughout these chapters, you'll learn how to truly unlock the potential of the public domain and turn it into a meaningful income stream. We'll start by demystifying what the public domain is, showing you just how much amazing content is waiting to be discovered. But it doesn't stop there. You'll be armed with practical tools and strategies for selecting, updating, and sharing these works in formats like eBooks, audiobooks, and even custom merchandise.

Importantly, you'll also discover how to evaluate the market potential of your chosen work, giving yourself the best chance of success from day one. Instead of wasting time on guesswork, you'll understand how to pinpoint in-demand content, stand out in a saturated market, and use platforms like Amazon to launch your projects with confidence.

No matter where you're starting from, whether you're a seasoned publisher, a total beginner, or someone just curious about new opportunities, this book provides a path that's both simple and effective. Starting with nothing but your imagination and a willingness to learn, you'll be surprised by what you can achieve.

Why This Book Will Work for You

This isn't just another theoretical guide filled with high-level ideas. Every chapter is packed with clear steps, real-life examples, and actionable advice designed to help you succeed. You'll learn the exact techniques others have used to profit from the public domain, and you'll have access to the same tools, platforms, and tricks they used.

What sets this program apart is simplicity. You don't need a lot of money, advanced tech skills, or even prior publishing experience to make this work. What you do need is a willingness to be creative, take steps, and commit to your projects.

By the time you finish this book, you won't just understand this process; you'll be ready to take action. You'll know where to find hidden gems in the public domain, how to attractively repackage them for today's audiences, and how to market them so they stand out in a crowded marketplace.

This Isn't Just About Money

Finally, and perhaps most importantly, this process isn't just about making money. The joy of working with public domain content is that it connects you to something greater. You're giving a new voice to works that deserve to live on. You're introducing these stories and creative ideas to fresh generations who might have otherwise never discovered them. It's about creativity, connection, and contribution, all wrapped into one rewarding experience.

The public domain is your untapped goldmine. This book is your roadmap to uncovering its riches. All that's left to do is take the first step. What comes next might just change everything.

Are you ready to unlock the treasure chest? Then turn the page, because the adventure begins now.

Chapter One

Understanding the Public Domain

What if I told you that some of the world's greatest creative works—from timeless novels to influential music compositions and historic speeches—are free for you to use, adapt, and repurpose however you like? Imagine holding in your hands the very stories, melodies, and ideas that sparked revolutions, inspired generations, and shaped entire cultures. No hidden fees, no complicated contracts, no endless legal negotiations. Just a wealth of creativity, ready and waiting for you to unlock its potential. Sounds almost too good to be true, doesn't it? But it isn't. That's the remarkable promise of the public domain.

The public domain isn't just a collection of forgotten works. It's a living, breathing reservoir of creativity, bursting with untapped potential. At its core, the public domain is a gift to humanity. When a work enters this hallowed space, it becomes truly free. It's like the ultimate creative toolkit handed down from the geniuses of the past, allowing you to take their ideas, words, images, and music and shape them into something new and exciting. Want to reimagine a literary classic as a modern-day graphic novel? Go for it. Have an idea to turn a historic speech into a podcast series? The floor is yours. Looking to transform breathtaking vintage artwork into a line of stationery or fashion? Nothing's stopping you. It's not just about consuming content. It's about becoming a creator, a partner in the ongoing life of these works.

Think about that freedom for a moment. No strings attached, no fine print. You can use the works as they are, or tweak, mold, and shape them to fit your vision. And here's what makes it even better: this creative freedom doesn't require you to be an established artist, a skilled entrepreneur, or someone with a massive budget. It's accessible to anyone who's curious, anyone who's passionate, anyone who sees the spark of possibility in something that's been overlooked. The public domain is the great equalizer, where the tools of inspiration and creation are placed into the hands of all who dare to grab hold of them.

Take music as an example. Some of the most famous compositions in history, like Beethoven's *Symphony No. 9* or Tchaikovsky's *Swan Lake*, belong to the public domain. If you're a musician, imagine remixing these classic pieces into a modern electronic album or using them to create stunning cinematic scores. Or consider the works of writers like Jane Austen or Charles Dickens. These giants of literature created stories that still resonate deeply with audiences today. Now picture yourself packaging Austen's *Pride and Prejudice* with fresh commentary for modern readers or designing an entirely new story inspired by its characters. The possibilities are as endless as your imagination.

But we're just scratching the surface here. Public domain content isn't limited to novels and symphonies. It spans an astonishing variety of media, from government-produced photographs of space exploration to maps, architectural designs, and even traditional folktales passed down through centuries. Each piece is a doorway into endless possibilities, and with public domain works, these doors are wide open.

Yet, to take full advantage of this incredible resource, you need to understand the rules that govern it. The public domain doesn't just happen by accident. It exists because copyright laws are designed with an end date in mind. Creative works don't stay locked up forever. Over time, they're released from their protected status and become a part of this shared cultural library. It's where yesterday's creations become today's raw materials for innovation and imagination.

This, perhaps, is the true magic of the public domain. It's not an archive of stagnant history, but a dynamic playground of infinite possibilities. It's an invitation to every dreamer, artist, and entrepreneur to take these works and make them their own. To discover and innovate. To give old ideas fresh life in a way that only you can.

But how can you step into this world and start making the most of it? First, you need the key to unlock it fully. And that key is understanding. Understanding how the public domain works, why it exists, and how you can separate the genuine treasure from what's still tied up in copyright's grasp. Whether you're here to spark a business, fuel your creativity, or simply explore its beauty, knowing how to access and use the public domain is the first step in a life-changing adventure.

This book is that key. The public domain offers you a blank canvas, an open book, a wide stage to express your ideas and reach new heights—but only if you're ready to open the door and step inside. Together, we'll explore this vast landscape, uncover opportunities hidden in plain sight, and transform what might seem complex into something simple, actionable, and incredibly rewarding.

What Is the Public Domain?

The term "public domain" refers to creative works that are not protected by copyright laws. It's like a shared cultural treasure chest, a creative well that anyone can draw from freely, without asking for permission or navigating complicated legal hurdles. These works span an incredible variety of media, including literature, music, films, art, maps, photography, and even scientific ideas. When a work enters the public domain, it becomes "owned" by all of us—not in a limiting sense, but in a way that invites everyone to reinterpret, reuse, and breathe new life into it.

To understand the significance of this, picture standing in a vast library. Imagine the shelves stocked not just with dusty books, but also with vivid paintings, orchestral scores, and reels of classic films. The best part? This library has no barriers. Every single piece in it is yours to use—for art, education, entertainment, business, or even just for fun. Artists turn these resources into new projects, museums use them to educate future generations, and entrepreneurs transform buried treasures into innovative products that resonate with modern audiences. It's not just a collection of outdated material; it's a living, vibrant pool of inspiration.

Take, for example, the works of William Shakespeare, whose plays, including *Romeo and Juliet* and *Hamlet*, have transcended centuries. Because their copyrights expired long ago, they are firmly in the public domain. This is why you can find Shakespeare's works in nearly every library and on countless websites. But more than that, the public domain status of these plays is what has enabled such creative freedom in reimagining them. Modern adaptations like the romantic teen comedy *10 Things I Hate About You* take inspiration from *The Taming of the Shrew*, giving it a fresh, contemporary spin while keeping its core themes alive. Similarly, Broadway classics like *West Side Story* breathe new life into *Romeo and Juliet*, setting the age-old story against the backdrop of urban gang rivalry. These adaptations demonstrate the immense power of public domain works to transcend time, culture, and genre.

The public domain doesn't end with literature. Consider the world of music. Works by legendary classical composers like Mozart, Beethoven, and Bach exist in the public domain because their copyrights long expired. Today, modern musicians often build on these timeless masterpieces, remixing them, sampling their melodies, or even transforming them into completely new compositions for film scores or contemporary pop music. Without the public domain, such creative bridges between the past and present wouldn't be possible.

Even films and visual art find their place in this collective resource. Silent screen gems such as Charlie Chaplin's *The Kid* or artwork from centuries ago, like the iconic pieces of the Renaissance, are free to be used and remixed by anyone. These works have inspired everything from multi-million dollar movies to vibrant fashion designs. Think about how film creators, designers, and illustrators take elements from these historic treasures and adapt them into something modern and unique. This cultural recycling not only preserves the heritage of the original works but also ensures they continue to remain relevant for contemporary and future audiences.

But the public domain isn't just for big-name adaptors or celebrated projects. It's a creative playground open to everyone. Whether you're a budding artist looking for raw material, a teacher seeking educational content, or an entrepreneur ready to launch a product, the public domain offers a wealth of resources waiting for you to explore. It allows creators, educators, and dreamers to connect with history in a way that's hands-on and participatory, placing the wonders of the past squarely in the present.

Ultimately, the public domain is more than a collection of old works. It's a vibrant, living resource that reflects humanity's collective achievements and invites everyone to participate in its ongoing story. Whether you're bringing a Shakespearean classic to the stage in a new way, remixing a Beethoven sonata with contemporary rhythms, or turning historic photographs into modern designs, the public domain is the canvas, and you are free to paint the next chapter. It's where creativity meets accessibility, and the possibility of reinvention becomes endless.

Why Do Works Enter the Public Domain?

The reasons why a work enters the public domain are rooted in both legal structures and creative generosity. This isn't a random process but rather a deliberate system designed to ensure that cultural, artistic, and intellectual creations eventually become accessible to all. A work's transition into the public domain is like handing down an heirloom to society, ensuring it remains not just a relic of the past but a tool for inspiration in the present. Let's break down the key reasons this happens and explore why they're so vital to the vibrancy of the public domain.

Copyright Expiration

Think of copyright like a lock on a treasure chest. The chest holds the rights to use, adapt, and distribute a creative work, and for a certain period, only the copyright owner has the key. But copyright isn't eternal. Just like that carton of milk in your fridge or the meter on a parking spot, it has an expiration date. Once that date passes, the lock disappears, and the treasure becomes accessible to everyone.

Under current U.S. copyright laws, works are protected for the life of the author plus 70 years. After that period ends, those works enter the public domain, where they're free for anyone to use, adapt, or reimagine. Take, for example, F. Scott Fitzgerald's classic novel *The Great Gatsby*. For decades, it was protected by copyright, meaning any adaptation required permission from the copyright holder. But in 2021, the copyright expired, and *The Great Gatsby* entered the public domain. Almost immediately, creators jumped at the chance to reimagine the story. New book retellings, musicals, and graphic novels emerged, fueled by Fitzgerald's imagery and themes but reinterpreted in fresh and exciting ways for modern audiences. This illustrates the beauty of copyright expiration—not as an ending, but as a new beginning.

It's important to note that while copyright in the U.S. generally lasts a long time, this length can vary depending on the country and the laws in place at the time the work was created. For example, in the U.S., any work published before 1923 is now safely in the public domain. Historical treasures like *Winnie-the-Pooh* (which entered the public domain in 2022) and early silent films are now part of this shared cultural reservoir, just waiting to inspire new audiences.

Government Works

Federal government works in the U.S. offer another fascinating pathway into the public domain. Unlike privately created works, which are protected by copyright, anything created by a federal government employee as part of their official duties is automatically in the public domain from the moment it's produced.

Why does this matter? Because some of the most iconic and widely used content comes from government sources. Take the unforgettable images captured by the Hubble Space Telescope, which are not just stunning but scientifically groundbreaking. Those jaw-dropping photos of galaxies and nebulae millions of light-years away are freely available for everyone to use. Photographers, educators, digital artists, and even entrepreneurs have turned these celestial vistas into coffee table books, educational materials, and even prints for home décor. And the best part? They didn't have to ask anyone for permission.

It's not just photographs. Government-generated content spans a wide range of media, from legal texts and laws to historical records and topographical maps. For instance, the content of landmark Supreme Court decisions is public domain, allowing researchers, educators, and content creators to interpret and share the material without restriction. This steady stream of public-access information adds richness to the public domain and ensures that valuable resources funded by taxpayers remain open and accessible to those same taxpayers.

Voluntary Waiver

The third pathway into the public domain is, perhaps, the most altruistic. Sometimes, creators voluntarily choose to dedicate their work to the public domain, making the conscious decision to set it free for all to use. While this isn't as common as copyright expiration, it's a powerful statement of generosity and a commitment to the idea that creativity thrives when it's shared.

There are many reasons a creator might make this choice. Some artists, writers, and musicians believe that their work is best used as a public resource, helping to educate, inspire, or entertain without barriers. For example, certain open-source projects, such as scientific research or educational tools, are created specifically to be part of the public domain, so they can reach the widest possible audience. Similarly, some creators see this as a way to maximize their work's cultural impact, knowing that its value lies not in exclusivity but in accessibility.

Creative Commons licenses, while not the same as the public domain, are one way that modern creators willingly release their work for public use, sometimes waiving most or all copyright protection. These licenses have allowed digital photographs, music, and scholarly articles to circulate freely, enriching everything from classrooms to online creators' toolkits. The ethos behind voluntary dedication reflects a modern belief that sharing ideas openly can lead to greater innovation and progress.

The Bigger Picture

Each of these pathways into the public domain serves a purpose, contributing to the richness and diversity of this shared cultural resource. Copyright expiration ensures that valuable creations don't linger behind locked doors forever. Government works remind us of the importance of open access to information created for public benefit. Voluntary dedication celebrates generosity and the belief that art and knowledge should be shared, not hoarded.

Together, these mechanisms sustain a timeless cycle. Past generations create, their works enrich society, and eventually, these works become seeds for future creators to cultivate into something new. The public domain isn't just a static repository of old material. It's a dynamic, evolving playground, one that invites you to participate in the ongoing story of human creativity. By understanding why works enter the public domain, you're not just learning about a legal process.

You're unlocking the door to a world brimming with opportunity, ready for you to explore.

Key Legal Concepts to Know

Before you start uncovering the treasures of the public domain, it's essential to understand a few foundational legal concepts. Don't worry, there's no need to dust off a law textbook or memorize complicated statutes. These are straightforward ideas that will help you grasp what's possible and keep you on the right side of the law as you begin creating, sharing, or repurposing works.

Copyright vs. Public Domain

Think of copyright as a bubble of protection that creators automatically receive when they make something original. This protection gives the creator exclusive rights to decide how their work is copied, shared, or adapted. Whether it's a book, a painting, a song, or a movie, copyright ensures the creator has control over their work—for as long as that bubble lasts.

But that "bubble" doesn't stay intact forever. Copyright comes with a built-in expiration date. Under current U.S. law, a work is typically protected for the life of the author plus 70 years. After that period ends, the copyright vanishes, and the work enters the public domain. Once that happens, anyone can use it freely without asking for permission or paying royalties. For instance, every note of Beethoven's symphonies is in the public domain, meaning you can remix them into a lo-fi chill playlist or use them in the background of a YouTube video without stressing about copyright infringement.

However, here's where people often get tripped up. Just because a work is "old" doesn't mean it's in the public domain yet. Books written in the 1940s, for example, might still be protected depending on specific copyright laws or extensions that apply. This is why verifying a work's copyright status is crucial before you jump into a creative reinterpretation. If you're unsure, don't just assume the work is free to use. Research can save you from potential legal headaches.

Fair Use

Fair use is one of those legal terms that sounds friendlier than it actually is. It allows you to use pieces of a copyrighted work without permission, but only in very specific circumstances. Imagine it as borrowing a teaspoon of sugar from your neighbor—not taking the whole bag. Fair use tends to apply when your use meets certain purposes like education, commentary, criticism, reporting, or parody. For example, a film reviewer showing a few clips to critique a movie is often protected under fair use. Similarly, a teacher sharing a passage from a copyrighted novel during a lecture might also qualify as fair use.

But here's the tricky part. Fair use isn't a black-and-white rule; it's more of a gray area. Courts analyze fair use based on factors like how much of the original work you're using, whether your use transforms it in some meaningful way, and whether it could harm the market for the original work. Unlike public domain works, which are entirely free of copyright constraints, fair use can be a slippery slope. If misapplied, it could land you in a lawsuit. This is why it's important to always tread carefully and understand the boundaries of this legal exception before relying on it.

Derivative Works

One of the most exciting aspects of the public domain is the freedom to create something entirely new from something old. This is where the idea of derivative works comes in. A derivative work is a fresh creation that's built on an existing one. Think of it as remixing or reimagining something classic to bring it into a whole new form. For example, turning a public domain novel like Mary Shelley's *Franken-stein* into a modern graphic novel or adapting it into a futuristic sci-fi screenplay would be considered creating derivative works.

Here's the fantastic news about derivative works and the public domain. Once a work is in the public domain, you have a blank check to create these new interpretations without the need for permission. Take *Alice's Adventures in Wonderland* by Lewis Carroll. It's been reimagined countless ways—from whimsical children's movies to dark, gritty video game adaptations. The same goes for *Sherlock Holmes*, whose adventures have spawned everything from TV dramas like *Sherlock* to playful animated comedies.

But it's important to remember that if you create a derivative work, the new work itself is copyrighted. This means you hold the rights to your personal spin on the material even though the original is free for anyone to use. For instance, if you illustrate a new version of the public domain poem *The Raven* by Edgar Allan Poe, your illustrations are protected by copyright—even though the poem itself belongs to everyone.

Why These Concepts Matter

Understanding these key legal concepts isn't just about staying out of trouble with copyright law; it's about equipping yourself with the confidence to explore the public domain boldly. Knowing the differences between copyright and the public domain, grasping the limits of fair use, and recognizing the opportunities of derivative works give you the tools you need to make informed, creative decisions.

The public domain is vast and full of opportunities, but those opportunities are best seized when approached with knowledge. Once you've got these foundational ideas under your belt, you're ready to unlock the creative potential of public domain content and start leaving your own mark on the world of art, business, and beyond.

Common Misconceptions

When it comes to the public domain, several myths and misunderstandings can lead to confusion. These misconceptions often stop people from confidently making use of public domain materials or, worse, result in unintentional copyright violations. Let's debunk these myths and set the record straight.

Myth 1: "If I find it online, it's in the public domain."

This is one of the most widespread misunderstandings about the public domain. The internet gives you access to an incredible wealth of information, art, music, and literature, but just because you can view or download something doesn't mean it's free to use. Copyright applies to works regardless of where you found them or how easy they were to access. For example, if you come across a photograph on someone's blog or a YouTube video, that work is still protected by copyright unless explicitly stated otherwise.

Think of it like walking into a museum. You can admire the paintings on the walls and even take photos of them (if allowed), but that doesn't mean you can walk out with one of the paintings or sell replicas without permission. Similarly, many copyrighted materials are uploaded for specific uses, like personal enjoyment or educational purposes, but they aren't automatically in the public domain. To avoid mistakes, always check the copyright status of a work or look for official public domain designations or Creative Commons licenses.

Myth 2: "Everything old is in the public domain."

It's tempting to think that age alone is enough to place a work in the public domain, but copyright laws aren't that simple. While older works are indeed more likely to have entered the public domain, they aren't guaranteed to be free of copyright. For instance, books published in the 1950s are still under copyright in the U.S. if they've been properly renewed, while others from the early 20th century are now public domain because their copyrights expired.

Think about *The Adventures of Tom Sawyer* by Mark Twain, which is freely available because its copyright expiration placed it in the public domain. Compare that to a mid-century novel like J.D. Salinger's *The Catcher in the Rye*, which remains under copyright today. While Salinger's book was published decades ago, it's still protected because copyright terms are tied to specific timelines, author lifespans, and renewal conditions.

To avoid confusion, pay attention to the year of publication and the country where the copyright applies. U.S. law, for instance, places works published before 1923 firmly in the public domain, but for works published after that, you'll need to dig a little deeper to verify their status.

Myth 3: "Only books are in the public domain."

When people think of the public domain, literature tends to come to mind first. After all, classic novels like *Pride and Prejudice* or *Moby-Dick* are staples of public domain archives. But the public domain isn't limited to books; it's a treasure trove of all types of creative works. Music, for example, offers exciting opportunities. The compositions of Beethoven, Mozart, and Bach are all in the public domain, meaning today's musicians can sample, remix, or reimagine their work without restriction.

Films and photography are also part of the public domain. Consider early black-and-white movies like Charlie Chaplin's *The Kid*, which are free to watch, share, and repurpose. Similarly, government-produced photographs, such as NASA's breathtaking images of space, are public domain works and widely used for education, art installations, and more.

Even scientific research and historical documents find a home in the public domain. Landmark resources like Isaac Newton's *Principia Mathematica* or research findings by government-funded projects are free to use, making them invaluable for educators, students, and innovators. Visual art, too, plays a role; paintings by the old masters, such as Leonardo da Vinci's *Mona Lisa* or Michelangelo's *Creation of Adam*, are no longer under copyright and can be reproduced or incorporated into creative projects.

By exploring beyond books, you'll find a universe of material waiting to be adapted, celebrated, and shared.

Myth 4: "You can do anything with public domain works."

While public domain works are free for everyone to use, there are still some nuances to consider. For instance, while the text of a public domain book like *Dracula* is free to use, specific modern editions with added commentary, illustrations, or new typesetting may still be protected by copyright. Similarly, a public domain song's composition might be available, but a modern recording of that song may have its own copyright.

Understanding the layers of copyright is crucial to avoid unintentionally using protected elements alongside public domain materials. When in doubt, investigate the specific version or adaptation of the work to ensure it's truly public domain through and through.

Separating Fact from Fiction

By addressing these misconceptions, you can confidently explore the public domain without fear of missteps. Think of the public domain as a shared library of creativity, one that requires a bit of research, respect for copyright, and curiosity to fully unlock its potential. Once you know the facts, the creative opportunities are limitless!

Why This Knowledge Matters

Understanding the public domain goes far beyond sidestepping legal pitfalls. It's about unlocking doors to a vast, untapped reservoir of creativity, history, and culture. At its core, this knowledge is a key that opens new worlds of possibility. Imagine taking timeless classics, iconic imagery, or groundbreaking historical documents and breathing fresh life into them. By knowing how the public domain works and why it exists, you gain access to an endless treasure chest of ideas waiting to be reinvented and shared with the world.

For creators, the public domain is a goldmine of inspiration. Picture adapting Edgar Allan Poe's haunting tales into a modern podcast series or crafting a children's picture book based on Aesop's timeless fables. Educators can enhance their lessons with vibrant public domain art, music, and literature, ensuring students connect deeply with history and culture. Meanwhile, entrepreneurs can seize opportunities to build entire businesses around public domain content. Think of how companies have used vintage travel posters, antique maps, or even forgotten music compositions to create best-selling prints, merchandise, and creative experiences.

This knowledge acts as a launching pad for innovation. Knowing the rules and tools of the public domain gives you the freedom to experiment and the confidence to explore uncharted territory. It's how filmmakers transformed Shakespeare's *Romeo and Juliet* into Baz Luhrmann's bold, stylized movie. It's how *Winnie-the-Pooh*, newly arrived in the public domain, is seeing quirky adaptations like horror-themed reimaginings alongside whimsical children's retellings. Armed with an understanding of the public domain, the opportunities before you truly become as limitless as your imagination.

There's an ocean of masterpieces, discoveries, and cultural landmarks just waiting to be revived, reshaped, and reintroduced to fresh audiences. And now that you've taken the first steps to understand what the public domain is and why it matters, you're on the brink of something exciting.

The next chapter will guide you through the practical steps of locating these hidden gems. You'll learn how to dig through archives, spot opportunities, and uncover high-value content ideal for your creative ventures. Your next big idea might already be waiting for you in the public domain. Grab your tools, sharpen your curiosity, and get ready to unearth treasures that will inspire the world.

Chapter Two

Finding Public Domain Books

Discovering the wealth of content available in the public domain is much more than running a quick internet search and hoping for the best. It's an intentional and rewarding process of digging deep into the history of literature, culture, and creativity. This process requires not only curiosity but also a clear strategy, the right tools, and a willingness to invest time and effort. True success comes from knowing where to search, understanding what types of works hold the most potential, and carefully verifying that the material is indeed in the public domain. When done methodically, this exploration becomes more than just research; it's an adventure into forgotten stories, timeless ideas, and untapped potential.

The first phase of this process involves research. This isn't just about typing keywords into a search engine but learning how to effectively use archives, repositories, and specialized databases. Platforms like Project Gutenberg, HathiTrust, and the Internet Archive are invaluable starting points, but they're only one part of the picture.

Exploring university library collections, national archives, or even dig-itized cultural libraries can open doors to rare works that are begging to be rediscovered. Your ability to unearth hidden gems depends on knowing where to look and being persistent enough to sift through vast collections of material.

Equally critical is prioritizing what to search for. Not every public domain work will hold commercial or creative value. Texts that have broad appeal, such as classic novels, can be reinvented in numerous ways, while niche works like vintage dictionaries, older how-to guides, or manuals on forgotten crafts can provide unique angles for special-ized audiences. The importance of goal-oriented exploration cannot be overstated. By identifying specific genres or themes before embark-ing on your search, you'll avoid feeling overwhelmed and ensure the works you uncover have relevance to your vision.

Finally, verifying the public domain status of a work is a meticulous but essential step. Copyright laws can be complex and vary across countries and time periods, so merely finding an old book doesn't mean it's free to use. Tools like the U.S. Copyright Catalog, digital renewal records, and international copyright databases offer clarity, helping you confirm whether a work is legally in the public domain. Ignoring this step could lead to costly legal issues, so diligence here pays off immensely.

When all these elements come together, you're left with not just a list of books, but a curated collection of possibilities. These works have the potential to inspire new ideas, be reimagined in fresh ways, and offer creative or financial rewards when shared with modern audi-ences. The process of discovering public domain content is, at heart, a creative endeavor in itself. Approaching it with care, enthusiasm, and a sense of discovery can turn dusty old texts into the foundation of something truly extraordinary.

Where to Start Your Search

The first step to finding public domain books is understanding where and how to begin your search. Some of the most valuable resources are hiding in plain sight, from physical libraries in your community to vast digital platforms accessible with just a few clicks. By knowing which tools and locations to explore, you can unlock a treasure trove of content brimming with creative potential.

Physical Libraries as Gateways to the Public Domain

Don't underestimate the power of your local public library. These institutions often house collections of older or rare books that have entered the public domain, sitting quietly on their shelves, waiting to be rediscovered. Many libraries also offer access to specialized archives or microfilm records, which can include first editions of historical or literary works from authors now in the public domain. Some libraries even partner with digital preservation initiatives, making it possible to access rare texts without traveling to see the originals.

University libraries can be equally, if not more, resourceful. Academic libraries often hold extensive collections of historic and artistic works, government publications, and classic literature. University archives may also include unique manuscripts or niche publications that could prove invaluable for creative use. Collaborating with librarians, curators, or researchers can help guide your search efficiently and reveal works you may not have considered.

The Role of Digital Libraries in Simplifying Discovery

Digital libraries have revolutionized the way public domain works can be accessed, removing the need to physically hunt down materials. Several major platforms stand out as essential starting points for finding and downloading public domain content.

Project Gutenberg

Project Gutenberg is a pioneer in the field of public domain accessibility. With over 60,000 free eBooks available, it offers a vast array of titles spanning genres like classics, history, and niche fiction. From Shakespeare's timeless sonnets to lesser-known 19th-century novellas, this digital library serves as a rich repository of high-quality literature, complete with options for various formats like ePub, Kindle, or HTML. One of its standout features is its focus on volunteer-driven proofreading, ensuring the texts are accurate and ready for immediate use.

HathiTrust Digital Library

HathiTrust is another excellent resource, particularly for researchers or those seeking specialized material. Its collection includes millions of digitized books and manuscripts from partner institutions around the world. While certain items require institutional access, many public domain works are freely available for download. HathiTrust is especially valuable for academic or niche subject areas, offering content that extends beyond well-trodden literary classics to rare texts you might not find elsewhere.

The Internet Archive

The Internet Archive goes beyond books, offering a dizzying variety of public domain content, including movies, music, audio recordings, and software. Its book collection encompasses everything from scientific treatises to vintage children's literature, making it an incredibly versatile tool for creators working across different types of media. The Internet Archive also includes a lending feature for works still under copyright, but its public domain resources remain freely accessible and universally rich.

Additional Digital Platforms and Specialized Collections

While the three platforms mentioned above are dominant players, they are by no means the only resources available. Google Books remains a strong option for identifying public domain works. Using its advanced search filters, you can target books that are free to use and legally in the public domain. The platform also lets you preview sections of certain books and provides helpful publication date information, making it easier to assess their utility.

National and regional digital libraries often represent hidden gems in the search for culturally significant or region-specific works. For instance, the British Library's digital archives include everything from early newspapers to historical atlases, while Europeana offers access to art, manuscripts, and literature from across Europe. These collections can serve as an incredible resource for projects tied to specific cultural or geographic themes.

Why Diversify Your Search Methods?

Relying on a mix of physical and digital resources ensures you won't miss valuable opportunities. Some works are digitized but not cataloged in mainstream archives, while others may exist only in physical form in your region. Diversifying your approach also allows you to uncover a wider range of content types, from popular classics that are easy to market to obscure texts that provide unique, niche appeal.

Unlocking the Potential Within Every Resource

Successfully navigating public domain resources requires more than knowing where to search. It demands a curious and investigative mindset, the ability to evaluate the value of the works you find, and a readiness to explore their potential uses. By fully leveraging libraries, both physical and digital, and tapping into platforms like Project Gutenberg, HathiTrust, and the Internet Archive, you'll be well-equipped to craft a collection of public domain books with potential for modern innovation. These works are waiting for creators like you to breathe new life into them. The rewards for your diligence could be immense, both creatively and professionally. Take the leap and start your search today.

Choosing High-Potential Genres and Niches

Not every public domain book holds equal potential for adaptation or reuse. A critical part of your research involves identifying the genres and niches that best align with your goals and audience preferences. Certain types of works naturally lend themselves to creative reinterpretation, offering the opportunity to repackage classic ideas in a modern, marketable format. Let's explore some of the most promising categories and what makes them valuable.

The Timeless Appeal of Classic Literature

Classic literature consistently proves to be a rich area for adaptation. Works by renowned authors like Jane Austen, Charles Dickens, and Mark Twain continue to captivate readers across generations. These authors bring universal themes, established audiences, and recognizable titles, making their books ideal starting points for creative reinvention. Their ability to connect with readers worldwide creates opportunities to present them in formats that appeal to new markets.

One of the most popular approaches to adapting classic literature is through graphic novels. Retelling beloved stories with vivid illustrations can breathe new life into old texts and appeal to younger or visual-oriented audiences. Another option is creating themed compilations based on specific themes or topics, such as a collection of Charles Dickens' Christmas tales or Jane Austen's romantic novels repositioned for special events like Valentine's Day. Interactive eBooks, which integrate animations, sound effects, or interactive questions, provide another way to modernize these works while enhancing user engagement.

Even lesser-known classics hold potential. Consider exploring works by authors who once enjoyed fame but have since faded from the mainstream literary spotlight. These "forgotten classics" may gain renewed popularity when reintroduced, particularly to readers seeking alternative content beyond commonly known titles.

Educational Content as a High-Value Resource

Public domain educational books also provide a broad spectrum of opportunities. Materials like outdated science primers, history textbooks tailored to past classroom curriculums, and early instructional guides often contain foundational knowledge that remains relevant. With a bit of creativity and updating, these works can be transformed into contemporary teaching resources.

For example, an old astronomy primer published in the early 20th century might include fascinating descriptions of celestial phenomena. While the scientific context can be modernized with the latest discoveries, the language and diagrams may serve as a nostalgic or unique teaching tool. Similarly, old history or geography textbooks with detailed maps and timelines can be revamped into visually striking coffee table books or integrated into homeschooling resources.

Educational adaptations can also expand beyond the classroom. Old business and self-improvement books, for instance, can be revised into streamlined manuals for modern professionals. Adding interactive elements like practice exercises or downloadable templates helps cater to today's tech-savvy learners.

Uncovering Potential in Niche Interests

One of the most exciting aspects of working with the public domain is rediscovering niche content that speaks to specific, passionate audiences. These niche interests range from vintage cooking guides to manuals on lost trades and crafts. By aligning your efforts with a clearly defined target group, you can connect with highly engaged users who value specialized, unique offerings.

Victorian-Era Cookbooks and Domestic Guides

Culinary history enthusiasts are one such audience drawn to the charm of old-world cooking. Victorian-era cookbooks brim with recipes, kitchen tips, and ingredients that reflect the cultural and culinary practices of their time. Modern creators can adapt these books by translating the measurements, updating techniques for modern kitchens, or pairing recipes with historical anecdotes to create a sense of nostalgia and connection.

Old domestic guides, such as household management books, fit well into this category, too. They offer a fascinating look into the domestic norms and wisdom of earlier generations, which can appeal to modern readers interested in minimalism, sustainable living, or historical lifestyles.

Manuals on Lost Crafts and Skills

Another niche ripe for rediscovery lies in manuals teaching forgotten crafts and skills. Topics such as dressmaking, woodworking, gardening, and metalworking often feature in vintage instructional guides with meticulous step-by-step details. These texts hold value for niche audiences, including hobbyists and makers passionate about reviving traditional methods. Adding modern commentary or video tutorials can elevate these into premium products for today's DIY community.

Self-Help and Spiritual Guidance

Public domain self-help books and spiritual guides from the late 19th to early 20th centuries also resonate with readers seeking timeless wisdom. These older works often emphasize universal principles of personal growth and self-discovery, which can be reframed and contextualized for modern audiences. For example, adapting a vintage self-help book into a sleek motivational journal or mindfulness app bridges the gap between historical insight and contemporary demand.

Aligning with Audience Preferences

The key to success in any genre lies in understanding audience preferences and aligning your adaptations with their expectations. This involves researching trends in publishing, examining what resonates within various demographics, and identifying gaps that your adaptations could fill. If you're targeting general readers, stick to evergreen subjects with broad appeal, like romance or adventure. For niche audiences, lean into the unique elements that make these materials stand out, such as historical authenticity or rare, specialized knowledge.

At its core, choosing high-potential genres and niches is about uncovering the hidden gems that balance creative excitement with market appeal. By focusing on areas like classic literature, educational resources, and niche topics, you can take full advantage of the public domain's rich offerings, creating something that not only honors the past but thrives in the present.

Verifying a Book's Public Domain Status

After identifying works with potential, your next task is confirming their public domain status. This step is critical to avoid copyright infringement and legal complications. While the general rule in the United States is that works published before 1923 are in the public domain, the nuances of copyright law can sometimes muddy the waters. Various factors, such as copyright renewal statuses, contributions by later editors, or added illustrations, can complicate a work's legal status.

Understanding the Basics of Copyright Law and Exceptions

The foundation of public domain status often lies in copyright law timelines. Under U.S. copyright law, works published before January 1, 1923, are generally considered public domain. However, works published after this date may also qualify, depending on whether copyright renewals were filed or whether the work fell into the public domain under previous laws. For modern creators, understanding these dates is essential when selecting material for reuse.

Exceptions occur frequently. A classic work from 1915 may seem to be public domain, but if it was republished with substantial revisions or new illustrations by another contributor in the 1950s, those additions may still be under copyright. Similarly, translations create additional challenges; while the original text might belong to the public domain, the translation often holds separate copyright protections. Always proceed with caution when dealing with materials that have been altered or repurposed over time.

Tools and Resources for Verifying Public Domain Status

Several tools and resources are available to help you verify whether a book is truly in the public domain. These platforms provide critical data to simplify your research and ensure legal compliance.

The U.S. Copyright Catalog

The U.S. Copyright Catalog, managed by the Library of Congress, is an invaluable resource for identifying copyright details for works published in the United States. This database lists historical records of copyright registrations and renewal filings that can clarify the status of older texts. By searching with a book's title, author name, or publication date, you can determine whether its copyright was renewed or allowed to lapse.

International Copyright Databases

For works created outside the United States, international copyright databases can provide essential information. Platforms like WIPO's (World Intellectual Property Organization) global copyright database offer tools for understanding copyright rules across different nations. It's important to remember that copyright laws vary significantly by country, so works that are public domain in one region may still be protected in another.

Additional Resources and Techniques

Platforms like HathiTrust and the Internet Archive often label public domain works, but creators should independently verify these claims to stay safe. A book flagged as public domain on one platform may not account for unique situations, such as protected annotations or recent republishing. Additionally, consulting with copyright experts, online communities focused on public domain publishing, or legal advisors can provide added clarity when needed.

Examples of Potential Complications

Revised editions and translations are some of the most common areas where complications arise. For example, suppose you've identified an

1890 edition of *Pride and Prejudice* with added illustrations from 1985. While the original novel resides firmly in the public domain, those illustrations almost certainly do not. Similarly, a French translation of Mark Twain's *The Adventures of Tom Sawyer* published in 1950 may carry active copyright protections on the translation, even though the original English text has long been public domain.

Another scenario involves anthologies that gather multiple public domain works. The original texts might be public domain, but a modern editor's notes, commentary, or prefatory material may hold separate copyright protections. It's best to access and work from the oldest possible version of the book (one devoid of newer contributions) to avoid these issues.

Practical Advice for Ensuring Compliance

To ensure you're legally in the clear, follow a few best practices. First, wherever possible, opt to use the original version of a text. Avoid editions with later additions, revised content, or new formatting. Tools like Project Gutenberg or original facsimiles available through HathiTrust can help provide access to unaltered works.

Additionally, make use of legally robust disclaimers if you include any questionable material in your project. While this won't override copyright issues, it can show good faith in your research process. Finally, if you're unsure about the status of a work, consult legal professionals with intellectual property expertise. The stakes for copyright misuse are high, so investing time in thorough research is always worth it.

Safeguarding Your Projects

Verifying a book's public domain status may seem tedious, but it's a crucial step to protect your creative efforts. By carefully navigating copyright nuances, diligently using verification tools, and understanding potential complications, you'll set a solid foundation for successfully working with public domain materials. With a little extra effort, you can confidently transform forgotten works into fresh, impactful creations without legal risks holding you back.

A New Way to See the Public Domain

The public domain is much more than an archive of old texts; it's a treasure trove of forgotten stories, ideas, and knowledge waiting to be rediscovered. By mastering the art of identifying and utilizing public domain works, you don't just gain access to content; you unlock opportunities to create something entirely new. You tap into a wellspring of possibilities that can be reinterpreted, modernized, and shared with eager audiences seeking refreshing and meaningful experiences.

Rediscovering Timeless Treasures

Imagine holding a century-old cookbook that captures the culinary traditions of an era long past or stumbling upon literary classics whose themes still resonate with today's world. These works offer us more than nostalgia—they give us context, history, and an insight into human nature that transcends time. Rediscovering these treasures allows us to see them through a new lens, identifying the universal truths and unique elements embedded within, ready to be reimagined for modern readers, learners, and creators.

When you uncover a forgotten text, it becomes an invitation to creativity. For example, a vintage gardening guide can inspire a modern audience through a beautifully designed adaptation for sustainable living, or a historical romance novel could make its way into a contemporary graphic novel series. The public domain is a mirror of our cultural heritage, and every story or idea within it has the potential to find new life with the right perspective.

Reimagining for the Modern Marketplace

The power of the public domain lies not just in what you find but in how you choose to bring it to life for today's audience. Your creativity is the bridge between the past and the present. With subtle updates, visual redesigns, or digital enhancements, you can take works that may seem outdated and make them relevant again. A simple instructional manual from the past can become an engaging digital resource. A compilation of moral tales can transform into an audiobook series perfect for families and classrooms.

These transformation opportunities extend beyond traditional publishing. Public domain content can form the foundation of podcasts, interactive apps, self-help workbooks, niche courses, or themed merchandise. The entrepreneurial applications are endless, limited only by your imagination and dedication. The public domain doesn't simply offer content; it provides a springboard for countless creative and business ventures.

A World of Possibility Awaits

Mastering the use of the public domain offers more than personal enrichment; it opens doors to unexplored pathways for creativity and entrepreneurship. With every work you uncover and reinvent, you're contributing to the preservation and evolution of ideas that continue to shape our world. The public domain stands as a reminder that creativity is cyclical and collaborative—that new innovation often grows from the seeds of the past.

By now, you've learned how to find and access public domain content, sparking inspiration and uncovering the raw materials for something extraordinary. The foundation is in place, and you're ready to take the next step. The following chapter will guide you through evaluating the market potential of the works you've discovered, helping you determine how to choose, shape, and position your content for modern audiences. The public domain is your canvas; now it's time to paint the picture.

Chapter Three

Evaluating Market Potential

The public domain is a vast reservoir of untapped potential, offering countless works that span genres, eras, and cultures. From timeless literary classics to forgotten niche treasures, the opportunities for creators and entrepreneurs are truly endless. Yet, success in this space isn't simply about accessing this treasure trove; it's about knowing how to mine it. Not all content carries the same potential, and the key to thriving in the public domain landscape lies in the ability to discern which works have the power to captivate today's audiences.

This pursuit isn't just about replication; it's about creativity and innovation. Recognizing in-demand material requires a blend of research, foresight, and an understanding of cultural shifts. With the right approach, you can uncover works that resonate deeply with modern readers, learners, or hobbyists, adapting them into formats that feel fresh and relevant. Whether it's revitalizing an 18th-century novel with contemporary illustrations, transforming century-old cookbooks into digital guides, or tailoring historical how-to manuals for today's DIY enthusiasts, the possibilities are limited only by your imagination.

This chapter is your guide to navigating the art and science of evaluating market potential. Together, we'll explore how to analyze trends, identify promising opportunities, and carve out unique angles that make your work stand out. By honing this vital skill, you'll not only unlock the full power of the public domain but also lay the foundation for impactful, profitable, and one-of-a-kind creations.

Recognizing In-Demand Content

The first step in evaluating market potential is understanding what readers, listeners, or consumers are seeking right now. While some works have enduring appeal that transcends generations, others gain momentum by aligning with cultural trends or current events. By understanding the difference between timeless and trend-driven material, and aligning content with the preferences of your target audience, you can make informed choices about which public domain works to repurpose.

Timeless vs. Trend-Driven Content

Certain works remain universally popular due to their enduring themes, characters, or cultural significance. These are the classics that never seem to lose their charm, regardless of era. Consider authors like William Shakespeare, whose plays explore the depths of human emotion, or Mary Shelley's *Frankenstein*, which continues to captivate readers intrigued by its mix of science, ethics, and horror. Works like these are reliable starting points for new projects, as their appeal requires little market validation. For instance, a modern graphic novel adaptation of *Romeo and Juliet* could easily attract a range of readers, from young adults to longtime fans of Shakespeare.

On the other hand, trend-driven content caters to cultural moments and shifting interests. Take the current popularity of mindfulness and self-improvement. While a relatively old concept, mindfulness has surged back into mainstream consciousness, creating a new demand for related resources. A century-old self-help or motivational book could thrive in this climate with simple updates or thoughtful repositioning. Similarly, as society places increasing emphasis on environmental consciousness, older gardening guides or homesteading manuals could be reintroduced as resources for sustainable living, breathing new life into what was once outdated material.

To strike a balance, evaluate whether a work has the potential to be both relevant now and evergreen over time. This dual appeal can give your project both immediate impact and long-term viability.

Aligning with Audience Needs

To maximize the success of your public domain project, you must align your content with the specific needs and desires of your intended audience. This requires identifying who your audience is and understanding what they value.

Identifying Target Audiences

Start by defining your audience categories. Ask yourself:

- Are you targeting students who need educational resources?

- Are families looking for wholesome or informative reading

material?

- Are there niche communities or hobbyists interested in specific topics, such as cooking, crafting, or history?

For instance, if you're considering revitalizing a collection of public domain fairy tales, your potential audience could include parents seeking bedtime stories, educators creating classroom materials, or even young adult readers interested in darker, unfiltered versions of these classics. Understanding your audience shapes how you present and package the content.

Practical Tips for Aligning Content

Once you've identified your audience, tailor your project to meet their explicit needs. Below are some practical approaches:

1. **Educational Alignment**

   Consider turning a historical text into an engaging, modern educational tool. For example, you could adapt a vintage science primer with updated illustrations, interactive quizzes, or teacher-friendly lesson plans. This would appeal not only to educators and homeschoolers but also to parents searching for supplementary learning materials.

2. **Family-Centric Content**

   Fairy tales, nursery rhymes, or classic children's literature always have an audience. For these works, enhanced illustrations, culturally diverse interpretations, or read-along audiobook versions could add appeal for family consumption. Imagine creating a beautifully illustrated and narrated digital version of the *Tales of Mother Goose* that appeals to tech-savvy parents and their children.

3. **Niche and Hobbyists' Interests**

   Fans of niche topics are often underserved by mainstream media, presenting a significant opportunity. A Victorian etiquette book could be redesigned for modern audiences interested in retro lifestyles, or an antique sewing guide could be turned into a step-by-step DIY manual for modern crafters. Providing practical value to niche audiences ensures your project has a dedicated and engaged user base.

4. **Cultural Relevance**

   Some themes speak to universal experiences but can also be made more culturally relevant with minor adaptations. For example, you could adapt a collection of historical speeches to include context about their impact on modern movements like women's rights or civil rights. By doing so, you contextualize seemingly outdated material for today's audience.

Where Timeless and Trend-Driven Content Intersect

Though some works are purely timeless and others purely trend-driven, the most impactful projects often sit at the intersection of these categories. For example, a collection of Aesop's Fables may hold timeless moral lessons, but if marketed as a resource for teaching ethical decision-making in business, it becomes newly relevant to trend-conscious professionals.

Moving Forward

Recognizing in-demand content is ultimately about blending awareness of market trends with creativity and a deep understanding of your audience. Whether you're modernizing a well-loved classic or bringing an obscure work back to life for a niche group, the possibilities within the public domain are vast. Targeting both what people need and what they are excited to discover will ensure your projects resonate while setting you apart from the crowd.

Analyzing Trends with Modern Tools

Understanding what audiences want is key to creating successful public domain projects. Thankfully, a variety of tools can help you explore market demand, uncover trending topics, and refine your approach. From identifying popular search queries to analyzing competitor success, these tools provide invaluable insights into the preferences of your potential audience. Here's how to use them effectively:

Google Trends

Google Trends is a powerful resource for gauging the popularity of search terms over time. Start by brainstorming keywords related to your potential project. For instance, if you're considering revitalizing a Victorian-era cookbook, search "vintage recipes," "historical cooking," or even "old-fashioned meals." Google Trends will show how interest in these terms has fluctuated over months and years.

You can also explore regional data. For example, an upward trend in "homesteading skills" searches in rural regions might indicate an interest in repurposed vintage self-sufficiency manuals. Use the "related queries" feature to uncover additional keywords worth exploring. Comparing terms like "antique cookbooks" and "retro recipes" could help refine your angle and choose the most effective language for marketing.

Amazon Bestsellers and Reviews

Amazon provides windows into audience preferences through its bestseller lists and customer feedback. To start, browse categories or genres related to your public domain project. For example:

- Seek out the top-performing titles in "Classic Literature Adaptations" or "Self-Help and Motivational Books."

- Look for trends around updated versions of public domain works, such as annotated editions, modern translations, or illustrated releases.

Pay close attention to customer reviews, as they often reveal unmet needs. For instance, if multiple buyers mention that an edition was difficult to read due to outdated language or poor formatting, these complaints signal opportunities for improvement. Incorporating clear, modern formatting or reader-friendly illustrations could distinguish your version.

Amazon's "Customers who bought this also bought" section is another helpful tool. It can identify adjacent niches that might broaden your scope, such as pairing a vintage herbal remedies guide with an updated book on modern herbal practices.

Social Media Listening

Social media platforms like Twitter, Instagram, and TikTok have become vital tools for trend analysis. Use hashtags and keywords to monitor conversations around topics linked to your project. For example:

- Search for terms like #booktok, #classicbooks, or #publicdomainworks on TikTok and see what's trending.

- Observe book-related hashtags on Instagram to uncover popular literary photography trends, such as aesthetically pleasing editions or engaging infographics about classic authors.

- On Twitter, keep up with cultural movements or anniversaries that may revive interest in certain public domain works. For instance, the 200th anniversary of a famous author's birth could spark renewed curiosity in their writings.

Social media influencers also offer crucial perspectives. Influencers who focus on niche subjects, like historical fiction or vintage design, often expose gaps in the market or specific audience preferences. Collaborating with them as part of your marketing plan could boost your project's visibility.

Niche Forums and Communities

Specialized forums, Reddit communities, and Facebook groups provide rich insights into what enthusiasts value. For example:

- Join subreddits like r/books, r/writing, or r/classiclit to understand what modern audiences think about specific genres or styles.

- Participate in communities such as Vintage Sewing Patterns (a group for sewing enthusiasts) or forums for local history buffs. This can guide you when repurposing specialized public domain content like antique craft manuals or historical essays.

- Observe community discussions about how older works might lack modern relevance, then determine how you could innovate while respecting the original's charm.

Interactive engagement in these spaces not only reveals audience preferences but also helps build relationships with potential users or advocates of your work.

Keyword Research and Planning Tools

While Google Trends is useful for exploring general popularity, dedicated keyword planners like Google Keyword Planner or third-party tools such as Ahrefs or SEMrush are essential for deeper analysis. These platforms allow you to:

- Identify keywords with high search volume but relatively little competition, offering the best opportunities for growth.

- Analyze seasonal trends. Keywords like "holiday baking recipes" might spike during the winter months, signaling optimal times for promoting repackaged cookbooks.

- Discover long-tail keywords like "step-by-step guide to Victorian etiquette" that reflect specific user intents, helping you create highly targeted content.

This kind of data-driven approach can refine everything from your project's focus to its online discoverability.

Competitor Analysis

Studying how others have successfully adapted public domain works can provide a roadmap for your own efforts. For example:

- Search platforms like Amazon or Etsy for projects similar to yours. Are pastel-colored reprints of literary classics outselling monochromatic ones? Are abridged versions more popular than unaltered full sets?

- Examine pricing strategies. Does demand shift noticeably between low-cost digital copies and premium hardcover editions with artistic covers?

- Identify gaps. If competitors haven't embraced multimedia adaptations of a book, like combining ad-free eBooks with bonus audio narrations, that might be your opportunity to stand out.

Competitor research helps identify both what's working and what's missing, allowing you to strategically position your project.

Practical Tips for Interpreting Data

Once you've gathered insights from these tools, the challenge is figuring out what to do with them. Here's how to apply your findings:

1. **Focus on Overlaps:** Look for recurring patterns between tools. If both Google Trends and Amazon reviews highlight growing interest in vintage self-help books, this alignment likely signals a promising market.

2. **Prioritize Specificity:** Broad keywords like "classic books" may have widespread interest but also significant competition. Go granular with niches (e.g., "Victorian etiquette guides for weddings") to better target audiences.

3. **Test Hypotheses:** Consider soft-launching a concept or limited edition to gauge interest before fully committing your resources. Social media polls or crowdfunding platforms make great testing grounds.

4. **Adjust as Needed:** Trends evolve. The insights you gather during the research phase should be revisited periodically to ensure you're still meeting market demands.

Moving Forward With Confidence

By leveraging modern tools to analyze trends, you equip yourself with the knowledge to align your public domain projects with audience demands. Whether it's identifying a niche, refining your approach, or uncovering new opportunities, these resources give you the edge needed to succeed. With actionable insights in hand, the path from idea to impactful creation becomes even clearer.

Case Studies of Successful Public Domain Projects

Examining real-world success stories can provide valuable insights and inspiration for your own public domain ventures. These case studies highlight the creative processes, challenges, and winning strategies behind some outstanding public domain adaptations.

Example 1: Revitalizing Classic Literature – *Pride and Prejudice* as a Graphic Novel

A team of creators reimagined Jane Austen's *Pride and Prejudice* as a graphic novel designed to appeal to a younger, visual-oriented audience. The creators retained the novel's core themes and timeless storytelling but used vibrant, contemporary illustrations to make the drama between Elizabeth Bennet and Mr. Darcy accessible to modern readers.

Challenges and Solutions: One major challenge was balancing fidelity to the original text with the need to streamline the story for the graphic novel format. The team meticulously selected key scenes that carried the heart of the narrative while condensing less critical subplots. Additionally, they faced skepticism from traditionalists who felt the project would detract from Austen's masterpiece. To address this, the creators presented their adaptation as a gateway for young readers to discover classic literature in a fresh format.

Marketing Strategy: A crowdfunding campaign on Kickstarter was essential in generating both funds and buzz. The creators shared early sketches and concept art on social media to build excitement and partnered with influencers in the comic book and literary communities. Post-launch, partnerships with schools and libraries further expanded their reach, proving the project's academic and cultural value.

The result was not only a fully funded project but also a bestseller across digital comic platforms, reaching diverse audiences and reigniting interest in Austen's work.

Example 2: Repackaging for Educational Use – *Grimm's Fairy Tales* Adapted for Writing Classes

An entrepreneur saw an opportunity to transform the timeless *Grimm's Fairy Tales* into a curriculum for creative writing students. The project involved annotating the original tales with prompts, challenges, and workshops aimed at helping students develop storytelling and analytical skills.

Creative Process and Challenges: While the core of the project relied on public domain texts, the creator needed to ensure the annotations and activities added real value. This required extensive collaboration with educators and students to design exercises that aligned with learning objectives. One challenge was overcoming the perception of the tales as merely children's literature. The creator reframed the stories as foundational examples of narrative structure, archetypes, and moral complexity.

Marketing Strategy: The project was marketed directly to educators and homeschooling communities through webinars, teaching conferences, and targeted ads on platforms like Pinterest and Facebook. The creator also launched a companion website with free resources to further attract teachers and parents. By positioning the adaptation as a teaching tool instead of just a collection of stories, the entrepreneur opened up a lucrative niche and established a reliable customer base.

The success of this project demonstrated how public domain works could evolve into highly specific, practical resources for niche markets.

Example 3: Creating Modern Niches – A Vintage Cocktail Guide

A vintage cocktail guide from the early 1900s was given a stylish makeover, transforming it into a high-end coffee table book that celebrated both history and craftsmanship. The publisher added historical context about Prohibition-era America, updated measurements for today's bartenders, and paired the recipes with stunning modern photography.

Creative Process and Challenges: The biggest challenge for this project was competing with other cocktail books in an already saturated market. The team overcame this by emphasizing the guide's unique historical angle, marketing it as a collector's item rather than an everyday recipe book. Collaborating with a professional photographer lent the project an upscale feel, and the final product was printed on high-quality paper with a vintage-inspired design to appeal to cocktail enthusiasts and gift buyers alike.

Marketing Strategy: The publisher initially launched the book through boutique bookstores, bars, and online e-commerce platforms aimed at foodies and history buffs. They also partnered with social media influencers in the cocktail space to spark conversations about the guide's rich history. Limited-edition releases, including a luxury box set with artisanal bar tools, created exclusivity and drove up demand.

The first print run sold out quickly, leading to subsequent editions and spin-off merchandise such as cocktail napkins and coasters featuring vintage illustrations from the guide.

Example 4: Multimedia Storytelling – *Alice's Adventures in Wonderland* as an Interactive Game

A tech-savvy creator turned *Alice's Adventures in Wonderland* into an interactive mobile game, blending classic storytelling with modern technology. Players could guide Alice through the whimsical world of Wonderland, with choices affecting how the story unfolded. The app included beautifully rendered animations and original soundtracks inspired by the story's iconic scenes.

Challenges and Solutions: The primary challenge was translating the written word into an engaging, interactive experience. To address this, the team collaborated with visual artists, voice actors, and musicians to create a richly immersive world while remaining true to Lewis Carroll's original tone. Licensing original artwork from earlier public domain versions provided a connection to the classic text.

Marketing Strategy: The app's launch focused heavily on digital channels, including partnerships with gaming influencers and advertisements on app stores. Free demo versions introduced users to Wonderland, while higher-tier purchases unlocked bonus content like Carroll's original illustrations and behind-the-scenes looks at the game's development.

This innovative project garnered critical acclaim, appealing to gamers, literary enthusiasts, and families alike, while proving that public domain works could find new relevance in the digital age.

Example 5: Digital-First Success – *Aesop's Fables* Reinvented as Animated Shorts

A content creator reimagined *Aesop's Fables* as a series of animated shorts optimized for platforms like YouTube and TikTok. The adaptations kept the original morals intact but updated the language, characters, and settings for a modern audience. For example, the tale of "The Tortoise and the Hare" was set in a bustling city, with the tortoise portrayed as a rideshare driver hustling to compete with the hare's flashy car.

Challenges and Solutions: One challenge was ensuring each short fit the fast-paced nature of modern video platforms while retaining the depth of the fable's message. To solve this, the creator limited each story to three minutes and focused on snappy, relatable dialogue. Animation costs were kept low by using simple yet colorful 2D designs.

Marketing Strategy: The series was distributed for free on YouTube, generating income through ad revenue and sponsorships. The creator also built a Patreon community where fans could access exclusive behind-the-scenes content, early access to new episodes, and merchandise like prints of the animated characters.

Within months, the series amassed millions of views, showcasing how even simple, timeless tales could thrive in a digital-first environment.

Lessons from Success

These case studies show that with creativity, strategic planning, and the right marketing tactics, public domain works can be transformed into innovative, highly profitable projects. Whether revitalizing classics or repurposing niche materials, the possibilities are as vast and varied as your imagination allows.

Avoiding Oversaturation and Finding Unique Angles

The public domain is a treasure trove, but you're not the only one who knows it. Some niches inevitably become crowded, making it crucial to differentiate your project in a way that grabs attention and creates lasting impact. By understanding common pitfalls and honing in on unique strategies, you can ensure your work stands out in even the most oversaturated markets.

Avoiding Common Pitfalls

One of the main challenges in public domain publishing is navigating areas that are either overcrowded or undervalued. Here's how to avoid two common issues:

Overused Classics:
It's tempting to turn to universally beloved works like Shakespeare or Dickens, but these classics are the first stop for many creators. This oversaturation can make it harder for your version to gain traction. If you do choose a popular title, look for ways to add value beyond the original. For instance:

- Create **interactive editions** where readers can click on words for definitions or annotations.

- Develop **audio companions** with immersive soundscapes or expert introductions that provide historical context.

- Present the text in an **unexpected format**, like a deck of flashcards for quick reference or games based on famous scenes.

Low-Quality Products:
A poorly designed or sloppily edited product can ruin your reputation before you even get started. Common mistakes include unformatted eBooks, lackluster cover designs, and outdated typefaces that fail to appeal to modern readers. Always prioritize quality by:

- Investing in professional design and editing.

- Enhancing your material with unique visuals, infographics, or detailed illustrations.

- Offering added convenience, like well-organized chapters,

hyperlinks in digital editions, or easy-to-read annotations.

High-quality production signals your professionalism and builds trust with your audience.

Finding Your Unique Angle

To rise above the competition, focus on ideas that break the mold. This doesn't mean reinventing the wheel but leveraging the originality inherent in the works you choose. Consider these strategies:

Focus on Subgenres and Niche Markets:
Sometimes the path to success is in narrowing your focus. For example:

- Instead of a standard re-release of *Alice's Adventures in Wonderland*, create a study guide tailored to psychology students that examines its themes of perception and reality.

- Transform unused vintage love poems into a collection marketed as wedding vow inspiration or personalized anniversary gifts.

- Repurpose early 20th-century travel guides as itineraries for eco-conscious adventurers seeking "vintage escapes."

Choosing a niche often means less competition and a more engaged, loyal audience.

Combine Genres or Formats Creatively:
Blending elements from different genres or formats can create something entirely new. For example:

- Combine the poetry of Emily Dickinson with modern nature photography to produce a coffee table book for art and literature lovers alike.

- Adapt Greek myths with modern self-help advice, positioning the tales as practical lessons in resilience, courage, or decision-making.

- Pair gothic horror classics like *Dracula* with a guide for hosting immersive murder mystery dinner parties.

Such crossovers not only appeal to multiple audiences but also provide a fresh take on familiar content.

Use Modern Technology:
Technology offers countless opportunities to innovate and present public domain works in unexpected ways. For instance:

- Develop an augmented reality (AR) app that brings scenes from classic tales to life by overlaying characters or settings on everyday environments. Imagine children "seeing" Cinderella's pumpkin carriage roll through their living room!

- Create virtual reality (VR) experiences where users can "explore" the moors of *Wuthering Heights* or walk through Dante's vision of the nine circles of hell.

- Publish interactive eBooks with quizzes, puzzles, or choose-your-own-adventure elements that transform reading into a dynamic activity.

By leveraging technology, you appeal to younger or more tech-savvy audiences while unlocking your creativity.

Identifying Oversaturated Markets

Before determining where to innovate, it's critical to research what's already out there. Keep these strategies in mind:

1. **Analyze Search Trends:**
   Use tools like Google Trends or Amazon's bestseller lists to identify areas that are flooding the market versus those where interest is emerging. For instance, while *Pride and Prejudice* is ubiquitous, there may be opportunities for obscure works by authors like Wilkie Collins or lesser-known Gothic writers.

2. **Assess Customer Complaints:**
   Scan reviews of competing products to uncover gaps. Buyers might complain about dull presentations, lack of context, or errors in text. Addressing these flaws in your version can give you the upper hand.

3. **Explore Specialized Communities:**
   Visit forums, subreddits, or Facebook groups tailored to niche interests. A group dedicated to steampunk culture or medieval reenactments might crave unique public domain content related to those themes.

4. **Monitor Popular Influencers:**
   Follow influencers on platforms like TikTok or Instagram who discuss literature, creativity, or hobbies. They often highlight trends and underserved topics, which can inspire your next project.

Examples of Unique Approaches

Here are some examples to spark your thinking:

- **Nostalgia Meets Utility:** Repackage public domain DIY

guides or home economics textbooks as modern-day life skills manuals for a self-reliant audience seeking tips on sustainable living.

- **Cultural Adaptation:** Collaborate with translators and cultural advisors to adapt European fairy tales for audiences in Asia or South America by incorporating regional references or visuals.

- **Customizable Editions:** Offer print-on-demand books with options for personal dedications, choice of cover designs, or additional forewords tailored to specific groups, such as educators or book clubs.

Leaning Into Creativity

Avoiding oversaturation and standing out in the world of public domain publishing isn't about avoiding popular works entirely; it's about how you breathe new life into them. By targeting overlooked areas, melding genres, and weaving in your personal ideas, you can ensure your projects are both innovative and profitable. With the right angle, even the most well-trodden public domain ground can feel fresh and full of potential.

Your Path Forward

Evaluating market potential is both a science and an art. By leveraging tools like trend analysis, understanding audience preferences, and learning from successful case studies, you can better position yourself to choose the right projects. Remember, the real value lies not only in what you find but also in how you adapt and present it. There's plenty of room to make your mark in the world of public domain publishing—as long as you do the research and find your unique voice.

Revitalizing and Repackaging Public Domain Content

Revitalizing and repackaging public domain content is both an art and a craft, requiring a delicate balance of creativity and strategy to transform timeless works into something fresh and captivating for today's audiences. It's not just about reworking what already exists; it's about reimagining it in a way that honors the original while introducing modern twists that make it more approachable, relatable, and relevant. This process breathes new life into written works that may have been overlooked or forgotten, enabling them to once again captivate readers across generations and cultures. By modernizing language, enhancing aesthetics, and revising structural elements to suit current tastes, you can effectively carve out a unique space in the marketplace, far removed from competitors who focus solely on original creations.

Modernizing language is one of the core pillars of revitalization. Many public domain texts are brilliant in their storytelling or educational value but fall short of connecting with modern readers due to dated vocabulary, dense sentence structures, or archaic expressions that feel inaccessible today. Take, for example, the works of Charles Dickens. While his stories explore universal themes of class, family, and morality, his writing can be challenging for contemporary readers unused to Victorian-era prose. By simplifying complex passages, adjusting pacing, or translating unfamiliar terms into plain English, his works become easier to digest without diminishing their power. The importance of this approach lies in understanding that readers want engaging content without having to fight through language barriers.

Aesthetics also play a pivotal role in repackaging content. Modern readers are often visually driven, which has led to the rising popularity of illustrated and graphically enhanced editions of classic works. The "Alice's Adventures in Wonderland" anniversary editions, for instance, frequently include vivid new illustrations that capture the whimsy of Lewis Carroll's world while updating its style for a modern audience. Similarly, repackaging historical texts with sleek, minimalist cover designs or bold typography can strongly appeal to today's book-buying trends, where presentation greatly influences perceived value. Enhancing the visual experience, whether through hiring contemporary artists or learning to use design tools yourself, can help a once-dusty classic jump off the bookshelf or stand out in an online catalog.

Adapting the structure of public domain content is another powerful way to make it resonate with modern audiences. Many older books have pacing that feels slow or inconsistent to readers familiar with today's fast-paced storytelling norms. Adjusting the flow, breaking up lengthy paragraphs, or even presenting key sections as sidebars or pull-outs creates a more dynamic reading experience. For example, cookbooks or instructional guides originally written in the early-20th-century often follow a dense narrative style that doesn't easily translate into actionable steps. By restructuring these works into modern recipes, step-by-step guides, or visually engaging info-graphics, creators can attract a far broader demographic, such as busy professionals or tech-savvy young readers who prioritize clarity and immediacy.

Success in revitalization also depends on understanding and adapting to audience preferences. Readers today aren't homogenous; they come with diverse tastes, needs, and expectations. A romance reader might prefer public domain love stories like "Jane Eyre" to include a highly emotional, dramatized introduction, while a sci-fi audience might be particularly drawn to republished vintage pulp fiction re-branded with futuristic covers and supplementary materials that connect classic ideas to contemporary tech culture. A prime example of understanding audience demand can be seen in the resurgence of fairy tales for adults, with classic folklore like the Brothers Grimm stories being revitalized through darker, mature retellings in print and streaming media.

One of the best examples of how effective revitalization and repackaging can be is the enduring success of William Shakespeare's works. His plays have been adapted and modernized countless times, taking forms as varied as musicals like "West Side Story" (based on "Romeo and Juliet") to modern Australian English translations for young readers. These updates amplify his universal themes while making them feel fresh and relevant for their respective audiences. Consider another example in the form of "Pride and Prejudice," which was cleverly reframed into a modern-day context with the wildly popular romantic comedy "Bride and Prejudice," proving that reinventing established classics can yield commercial success in new mediums.

By approaching revitalization with a blend of creativity and market awareness, you not only ensure that these timeless works find new audiences, but also position your reimagined product as something truly distinctive. Every choice, whether it's simplifying language, incorporating modern visuals, or tailoring the content for niche readers, builds upon the legacy of the original work while showcasing your ability to innovate. Through understanding the pulse of the contemporary audience and putting genuine effort into your enhancements, revitalized public domain works don't simply serve as recycled ideas; they stand tall as engaging, profitable ventures that can resonate for years to come.

The Art of Giving Old Content New Life

Revitalizing content begins with a deep understanding of the essence of the original work. This essence is what made it resonate with its readers in the first place, whether it was compelling characters, universal themes, or its unique storytelling voice. The goal is not to rewrite history but to reframe it so that it speaks to modern audiences. This delicate balance involves respecting the original creator's intent while enhancing elements that contemporary readers may find inaccessible or outdated.

Consider a classic novel from the early 1900s. While its central themes of love, resilience, or social dynamics may remain timeless, the language often feels foreign to modern readers. Long, winding sentences packed with archaic terms can create a barrier that prevents engagement. Modernization in this context is about breaking down those barriers. By simplifying complex phrases, adjusting sentence structures, and subtly substituting outdated expressions with more familiar ones, you allow the story to unfold naturally for today's audience. Yet, care must be taken to preserve the tone and style that defined the author's vision. For instance, in literary works like "Dracula," the gothic mood and eloquent narration are integral to the text's identity. Simplifying the prose too much could dilute the intensity of its atmosphere, so modernization must tread lightly, focusing on readability without reducing its richness.

A significant example of this is in the ongoing evolution of Jane Austen's works. Her novels, such as "Pride and Prejudice" and "Emma," explore human nature and relationships in ways that remain profoundly relevant. However, much of the humor or social critique in her writing can be esoteric to a modern reader unfamiliar with Regency England. Publishers often tackle this by including annotations that explain historical references, cultural nuances, or even the subtle puns Austen's original readers might have instantly grasped. Other efforts go beyond annotation, reshaping her stories for newer audiences. For example, modern retellings like "Pride and Prejudice and Zombies" cleverly combine the framework of her iconic romance with a genre that appeals to fans of horror and fantasy, showing how a classic can be reimagined in a completely new light. These adaptations often reach audiences who may never have considered reading Austen's work in its original form.

Another layer of bringing old content to life lies in considering how to bring greater accessibility. For instance, works by authors such as Mark Twain or Herman Melville are often retold with simplified phrasing or abridged versions designed for younger readers. These adaptations help to introduce younger generations to literary classics without overwhelming them with dense language or extended descriptions that may be more suitable for seasoned readers. The challenge is ensuring that these changes don't erode the integrity of the text. For example, Twain's wit or Melville's mastery of symbolism lose much of their impact if stripped down too far. The art lies in maintaining the narrative's essence while making it feel fresh and welcoming.

Modernizing old content isn't just about language, either. It involves updating contextual or cultural references that may feel irrelevant or even problematic to contemporary audiences. For instance, instructional guides or books containing outdated stereotypes or assumptions can be revised to better align with modern values and expectations. A cookbook from the Victorian era, for example, may still hold immense appeal due to its vintage recipes but might include ingredients that are either hard to source today or have fallen out of favor. A revised version can offer modern equivalent ingredients alongside notes about their historical authenticity for readers interested in understanding both worlds. These types of updates allow content to both educate and appeal to evolving preferences.

At its core, the process of giving old content new life depends on the audience you hope to reach. For literary purists, offering annotated versions or faithful reproductions with an improved layout might be enough. For a broader or younger audience, transforming the work into a visually rich illustrated edition might be the better approach. An excellent case study of this is the continued popularity of children's versions of "The Iliad" or "The Odyssey," where lush illustrations and simplified storytelling turn dense epics into magical adventures suitable for younger readers. Without such revitalization, these stories might remain untouched, confined to academic circles rather than embraced as universal treasures.

Ultimately, this process demands both care and creativity. The reverence you show for the original writing is just as important as the ingenuity you apply in adapting it. It's about creating a bridge between eras, one that enables timeless stories to continue inspiring and entertaining readers while ensuring they feel relevant rather than relics of a distant past. Revitalized public domain content, when handled with this balance in mind, achieves something extraordinary. It doesn't merely preserve history—it reinvents it with every passionate reader in mind.

Strategies for Repackaging Content

Once the content is revitalized, the next step is to determine how best to present it to audiences in a way that amplifies its appeal and accessibility. Repackaging is where imagination and market awareness intersect, offering limitless possibilities for transformation. It is about re-envisioning existing works as formats, designs, or experiences that align with current trends while still honoring their original essence. The presentation, visuals, and thematic framing make a significant impact on how audiences perceive public domain content. Crafting this stage thoughtfully allows a classic work to not only remain relevant but to thrive in modern marketplaces.

Illustrated Editions: Breathing Life Into Timeless Stories

One of the most impactful ways to repackage public domain content is through the creation of illustrated editions. Visuals have an inherent ability to deepen storytelling, engaging readers by providing an additional sensory connection. For example, imagine a richly illustrated edition of Grimm's Fairy Tales, with captivating full-color artwork drawing younger readers into the enchanting worlds of these age-old tales. The experience becomes more immersive, reducing the intimidating barrier that unadorned text might present.

Illustrated editions aren't just for children's books. There is a growing appetite among adult readers for graphic and visually enriched versions of literary classics, often tailored to specific genres like fantasy or horror. A moody, atmospheric reinterpretation of Robert Louis Stevenson's "The Strange Case of Dr. Jekyll and Mr. Hyde" with dark, gothic illustrations could appeal to fans of eerie, visually striking content. Whether collaborating with artists or leveraging modern design tools, adding visual elements transforms a traditional text into something dynamic and irresistible.

Annotated Guides for Greater Context and Depth

Another powerful strategy for repackaging is creating annotated guides. By adding layered commentary, historical insights, or practical observations, you breathe new relevance into the original text. Annotated editions provide readers with tools to engage deeply with a work, offering them a richer understanding of its context and nuances. For instance, "The Art of War" by Sun Tzu can be expanded into an annotated guide where each strategy is paired with modern applications for leadership, business, or personal growth, making its ancient wisdom accessible and actionable today.

Similarly, literary classics like Herman Melville's "Moby-Dick" can become treasure troves of cultural and historical significance through annotations. Insights into whaling practices of the time, philosophical undercurrents, or Melville's religious allegories can transform dense prose into a fascinating exploration for curious minds. The value of annotated versions lies in their ability to provide audiences with the tools they need to connect with and appreciate a text beyond its surface.

Thematic Compilations for New Perspectives

Themed compilations are an excellent way to offer a curated experience while broadening the appeal of public domain works. This approach not only expands the available content but draws readers in with a sense of intentionality. A compilation such as "Great Ghost Stories of the Victorian Age" might unite the gothic creations of Edgar Allan Poe, Mary Shelley, and Lord Dunsany within a harmonious framework. Featuring a unifying introduction or commentary, the collection helps readers explore shared motifs or contextual shifts across the stories.

Compilations are also perfect for connecting seemingly unrelated works around a fresh concept. For instance, a collection juxtaposing feminist essays from the 19th century with contemporary analysis could attract modern readers eager to see how discourse has evolved. The appeal of compilations often lies in their ability to make connections and present classic texts in a novel, cohesive fashion.

Hybrid Works: Reinventing Through Innovation

Perhaps the most inventive method of repackaging is creating hybrid works, blending elements of multiple public domain sources or combining them with original ideas to create something entirely unique. For example, an updated Victorian-era cookbook could include traditional recipes alongside modern substitutions and nutritional tips, appealing to both history enthusiasts and culinary adventurers. The hybrid approach allows creators to infuse traditional material with a modern twist, expanding its appeal while retaining its core essence.

Some hybrids go so far as to explore entirely new interpretations of familiar worlds. Writers have crafted prequels, sequels, or spin-offs rooted in public domain classics, such as revisiting the untold stories of minor characters or exploring alternate endings. These reinventions cater to audiences who value nostalgia but crave exciting new dimensions to beloved works.

New Formats for a Changing World

Public domain content also lends itself to adaptation into entirely new formats. Visual storytelling mediums, such as graphic novels, animations, or interactive apps, offer pathways to attract younger, tech-savvy audiences. A short story by H.P. Lovecraft, for instance, could be reimagined as a motion comic, where eerie soundtracks and dramatic visuals amplify the tension. Likewise, an immersive augmented reality experience inspired by the poetry of Emily Dickinson could combine fragments of text with dynamic environments, creating an entirely new way to "read" and engage with her work.

This strategy also includes adapting content for formats such as podcasts or audiobooks. With rising demand for narrated experiences, classics like "War and Peace" or "Les Misérables" could be converted into serialized episodes that break down complex narratives into manageable, compelling chapters, perfectly tailored to contemporary consumption habits.

Navigating Challenges in Repackaging

While repackaging offers endless possibilities, it also presents challenges. Moving too far from the original intent can alienate dedicated fans, while being overly cautious may prevent the material from capturing new attention. Striking a balance requires understanding audience tastes and staying informed about trends in media and culture. A thorough market analysis can help uncover opportunities for innovation, such as tailoring gothic classics for emerging audiobook enthusiasts or presenting ancient mythology in formats suitable for social media storytelling.

Transforming Timeless Works into Relevant Treasures

Repackaging public domain content is about seeing potential where others might not. Through illustrated editions, annotations, compilations, hybrids, and innovative formats, you can give classic works a fresh identity. By taking these steps with creativity and care, you breathe new energy into stories and concepts that might otherwise remain buried in obscurity. This creative process builds a bridge between eras, ensuring that timeless narratives continue to inspire and delight readers in a world that's forever changing.

Modernizing Language and Concepts Without Losing the Essence

Striking the right balance when modernizing content is an art form requiring both sensitivity and strategy. It's easy to be tempted by the idea of completely overhauling an older work into modern vernacular, but this can risk losing the very qualities that made the original so compelling. For a modern reader, the goal should not be to erase the past, but to create a bridge between eras. A skilled approach maintains the historic charm and character of the original while carefully addressing the parts of the language or concepts that pose genuine barriers to comprehension.

Language modernization, in particular, demands a delicate touch. Works like those of Shakespeare, for instance, are renowned for their poetic complexity, yet this complexity often alienates modern audiences unfamiliar with Elizabethan English. While purists may prefer unaltered editions of his plays, modern adaptations have found a way to coexist. "Plain English" versions of his works provide entry points for new readers, stripping away linguistic obstacles while leaving the integrity of the story intact. For example, phrases like "wherefore art thou Romeo?" become more accessible as "why are you Romeo?" The original intent and emotions shine through such changes, reminding audiences why these works continue to resonate.

Modernization isn't limited to literature. The same principles apply when dealing with instructional guides or reference material from earlier eras. Many works written in the 19th or early 20th centuries reference tools, techniques, or cultural norms far removed from today's realities. Revitalizing these texts requires thoughtful substitution rather than wholesale replacement. Consider, for example, a Victorian-era knitting manual that describes using unwieldy wooden needles and fibers like mohair. While adding historical context to these methods is invaluable, suggesting contemporary materials or tools, such as lightweight aluminum needles or synthetic yarn alternatives, allows readers to engage actively with the content. This dual approach retains authenticity but ensures usability.

One fascinating example of modernization done right is seen in updating culinary texts. A mid-20th-century cookbook might tout recipes heavily reliant on ingredients like lard or gelatin molds, both of which align less with modern tastes. By offering updated alternatives, such as using olive oil or incorporating fresh, plant-based options, these recipes can be repurposed for contemporary kitchens. Crucially, retaining the nostalgic tone of the original cookbook, perhaps through retro design elements or vintage commentary, preserves the charm of its era.

Modern concepts also face the challenge of preserving the intent behind now-outdated practices. Many instructional or philosophical texts discuss societal norms or gender roles that no longer align with today's values. Revitalizing these works requires carefully balancing modern sensibilities with a respect for the historical perspective. For example, texts from early suffragists or social reformers can have their core messages of equality and empowerment emphasized, reshaped for modern consumption without diluting their historical importance. A colonial-era pamphlet on women's domestic roles might seem restrictive by today's standards, yet it can serve as the backbone for a contemporary discussion on how those roles have evolved.

At its heart, the process of modernizing public domain content lies in understanding the audience. Different readers will have different expectations based on their preferences. While high school students might appreciate simplified versions of famous novels with added modern nuances, literary scholars may demand unaltered texts supplemented by footnotes. A popular modern interpretation of Jane Austen's work, for instance, may subtly edit or adapt her socially vibrant manners-of-the-time dialogue for clarity, but care is taken not to erase her wit and irony.

The key to success lies in selective editing. Language and concepts should only be changed when they present an obstacle rather than an opportunity to preserve authenticity. Annotation and context often offer viable alternatives to outright edits, allowing the original work to shine through while still making it broadly relatable. For example, historical treatises referencing bygone political structures can be paired with side-by-side modern interpretations that explain their relevance in today's systems of governance. This ensures that the reader retains the original depth while also receiving an accessible window into its concepts.

Ultimately, modernizing language and concepts without losing the essence of original works is about honoring the past while welcoming the present. By prioritizing clarity, usability, and respect for historical context, creators ensure that these texts remain living documents. The charm, intent, and wisdom encoded in these timeless creations become accessible anchors, both educating and resonating with new generations. This thoughtful balancing act ensures that modern audiences are not alienated yet still feel the richness and authenticity of the original work.

Creating Compilations and Hybrid Works

Creating compilations and hybrid works offers exciting opportunities to reimagine public domain content. By curating selections around a focused theme or blending storylines in innovative ways, you can deliver something fresh and imaginative while staying connected to the beloved foundations of classic works. Both approaches allow you to engage new audiences, breathe life into old ideas, and craft deeply memorable experiences.

Crafting Thematic Compilations

The key to an impactful compilation lies in selecting a unifying theme that not only connects the content but also speaks directly to your audience's interests or passions. Thematic compilations go beyond a simple aggregation of works; they provide a cohesive narrative or intellectual exploration. For instance, a collection like "The Essential Leadership Collection" could bring together writings by Benjamin Franklin, Napoleon Hill, and other influential thinkers, presenting timeless lessons on leadership, perseverance, and personal growth. By offering a preface that highlights the thematic ties across these authors' ideas, you help guide your readers and enhance their understanding of how these works intersect.

A thematic compilation also has the power to introduce lesser-known works alongside more celebrated ones, broadening the reader's exposure. For example, a collection of Gothic literature could feature familiar names like Edgar Allan Poe and Mary Shelley while introducing less mainstream authors like Ann Radcliffe or Sheridan Le Fanu. A thoughtful introduction detailing the evolution of the Gothic genre enriches the reader's experience, transforming the compilation into more than just a literary catalog but a broader cultural exploration. This strategy creates a strong connection with audiences who seek both depth and discovery.

Compilations targeting unique or niche themes, such as "Victorian Women Writers on Freedom and Constraint" or "Eco-Wisdom from the Public Domain," might pull together essays, stories, and poetry from diverse authors addressing similar ideas. Adding context through introductions or annotations ensures readers grasp the theme's enduring relevance. Such collections cater to modern audiences craving meaning and connection while still celebrating historical perspectives.

Experimenting with Hybrid Works

Hybrid works take creativity to the next level by merging old and new, offering limitless possibilities for rejuvenating public domain content. They are particularly powerful in storytelling, allowing you to reimagine classics with surprising twists or fresh perspectives. An excellent example of this approach is the addition of entirely new narratives to previously standalone classics, such as crafting a sequel to Mary Shelley's *Frankenstein*. Expanding on Frankenstein's monster's exile or exploring the moral dilemmas faced by Victor Frankenstein's descendants can provide fresh narrative layers while respecting the themes of the original text.

Hybridization also enables playful reimaginings of genre and tone. Consider "Pride and Prejudice and Zombies," where a modern sense of humor transforms Jane Austen's high society love story into an action-packed tale of survival during a zombie apocalypse. While satirical, the book preserves Austen's wit and commentary on societal norms, ensuring it feels grounded in its source material even as it takes wild creative liberties. Similarly, Gregory Maguire's *Wicked*, inspired by *The Wizard of Oz*, shifts focus to the perspective of the Wicked Witch, reinterpreting a familiar classic into an entirely original exploration of morality, power, and identity.

The possibilities for merging narratives are equally exciting. Imagine blending characters and plots from multiple public domain classics to construct an entirely new shared universe. What might happen if Victor Frankenstein's monster crossed paths with Sherlock Holmes to solve a murder mystery? What adventures could ensue if Alice from *Alice's Adventures in Wonderland* stumbled into a voyage aboard Captain Nemo's Nautilus? These mashups have the potential to combine nostalgia for beloved characters with captivating originality, opening up your work to readers intrigued by the unexpected.

Challenges and Strategic Considerations

Both compilations and hybrid works come with unique challenges. Curating works for compilations requires careful consideration of audience preferences and thematic relevance. Too broad a theme risks diluting the collection's impact, while an overly narrow focus might limit its appeal. The success of a compilation often lies in thoughtful curation, writing compelling introductions, and ensuring the selected works are accessible, relevant, and engaging for modern readers.

With hybrid works, creators must tread lightly around the original material to avoid alienating established fans. Successful hybrids strike a delicate balance between innovation and loyalty to the source. For example, altering core themes or drastically changing character traits can feel jarring or disrespectful to audiences deeply invested in the original. However, by focusing on enriching rather than rewriting or invalidating the original intent, you can strike a successful balance, offering fresh content while honoring historical roots.

Engaging Modern Audiences

At the core of both compilations and hybrid works is a focus on engaging today's readers in new and stimulating ways. Creative presentation is as important as the content itself. For instance, designing a visually stunning and stylish collection with contemporary typography and compelling cover art can attract audiences who might otherwise overlook older works. For a hybrid exploration, presenting the content as a graphic novel, digital experience, or dramatic podcast series can amplify its appeal to younger, tech-savvy consumers.

Additionally, the power of storytelling extends beyond the pages. For hybrid works, engaging promotions could include multimedia campaigns that elaborate on the creative process behind blending two classics. Compilations may benefit from curated packages, such as supplemental materials like reading guides, essays, or themed recipes, further immersing the reader into the world you've created.

Building Bridges with Creativity

Creating compilations and hybrid works is ultimately about tapping into a shared love for classic literature and rechanneling it through new avenues of creativity. By crafting compilations that weave together complementary pieces or by finding novel ways to reinterpret classic material through hybrids, you are not just preserving the past but enriching it for future generations. These forms of creative expression provide timeless works with new life, proving that even the most venerable stories and ideas have endless potential when viewed through the lens of innovation.

Practical Tips for Repackaging Success

Successful repackaging goes beyond simply reintroducing classic works; it demands a strategic approach that merges creativity, meticulous planning, and market awareness. To create compelling and profitable products, every element of presentation, formatting, and marketing must align to meet the needs and tastes of modern readers. By refining these details, you elevate the appeal and accessibility of public domain works, ensuring they resonate with contemporary audiences.

One of the most important aspects of repackaging is presentation. A high-quality cover design is not just an aesthetic choice; it determines the perceived value of a book at first glance. Readers often judge a book by its cover, so investing in strong visuals is critical. Choose modern, eye-catching designs that capture the tone and essence of the content within. For instance, a gothic literature collection featuring works by Edgar Allan Poe or Mary Shelley could use moody, atmospheric imagery. These visuals should appeal to fans of the genre while echoing the eerie suspense and darkness that define the narratives. Similarly, bright, colorful covers with whimsical illustrations might be perfect for children's literature, such as a repackaged edition of Rudyard Kipling's *The Jungle Book*. Striking the right balance between modern sensibilities and thematic relevance ensures your cover art attracts attention while staying faithful to the spirit of the work.

Formatting is another crucial area for success. Whether you're creating digital editions for e-readers or physical copies for bookstores, the layout should prioritize readability and functionality. For digital formats, ensure text flow is smooth, chapters are properly hyperlinked, and images, if included, render well on various devices. Physical editions benefit from clean typography, comfortable spacing, and durable bindings that add to their longevity. Including extra features like personalized introductions, detailed indexes, or accompanying digital content, such as downloadable audio readings, provides additional value and enriches the overall experience.

Equally vital is market research, which guides decisions on which works to focus on and how to position them effectively. Online platforms like Amazon or Goodreads can serve as invaluable tools for identifying market gaps and trends. For example, if illustrated editions of classic literature are in high demand, you could prioritize creating your own visually enhanced version of *Peter Pan* or *Alice's Adventures in Wonderland*. Similarly, niche markets like minimalist cookbook enthusiasts or true crime fans could inspire repackaging projects tailored specifically to their tastes. By staying attuned to these trends, you can refine your offerings to align with audience preferences, boosting your content's visibility and profitability.

Focusing on timeliness in repackaging efforts can provide you with an edge in competitive markets. If a new film adaptation of a well-known work is set to release, such as a production of *Little Women* or *Dracula*, timing the relaunch of an annotated or illustrated edition of the book to coincide with its premiere can capitalize on renewed interest. This synchronization fosters immediate relevance, capturing readers riding the wave of public awareness.

While market trends are important, creativity and imagination are equally integral to repackaging success. Beyond simply resurrecting texts, aim to provide a new perspective or experience that sets your work apart. For instance, turning a forgotten etiquette guide from the 1800s into a humorous coffee table book for modern audiences can transform dry material into delightful entertainment. Similarly, revamping a philosophical work, like Seneca's *Letters to Lucilius*, with modern analogies and design elements can appeal to readers seeking ancient wisdom with a relatable twist.

Engaging audiences goes hand in hand with crafting the work itself. A well-told story about your repackaging process can become a selling point in its own right. Sharing behind-the-scenes insights, such as how illustrations were created or why certain thematic decisions were made, fosters a deeper connection with your readers. Social media campaigns, blogs, or podcasts that guide audiences through your creative decisions add authenticity and invite them to participate in the narrative surrounding the revitalized work.

Ultimately, revitalizing and repackaging public domain content is a delicate balance between honoring the brilliance of the past and enhancing its relevance for today. Thoughtful presentation, meticulous formatting, market-informed choices, and bold creativity are your tools to breathe new life into aging texts, ensuring they captivate audiences in new and exciting ways. These efforts not only preserve history but empower it, creating cultural bridges that connect the timeless beauty of classic works with the dynamic tastes of modern readers. Through careful planning and a touch of imagination, forgotten treasures can evolve into contemporary gems cherished by entirely new audiences.

Chapter Five

Formats and Mediums for Success

The success of revitalizing public domain content often hinges on selecting the right format for your project. Choosing the right medium isn't just about functionality; it plays a crucial role in how the content resonates with your target audience and secures its place in the market. Today's publishers and creators have access to a wide array of distribution options and technologies that can transform classic works into engaging experiences, designed not only to preserve their timelessness but also to enhance their appeal in new and innovative ways. Formats such as eBooks, print editions, audiobooks, and experimental technologies like augmented reality each offer unique opportunities to connect with modern consumers, expanding the reach and profitability of public domain content in ways previously unimagined.

EBooks are an obvious starting point for bringing old texts into the digital age. They are not only cost-effective to produce but also highly adaptable to various devices, from e-readers to smartphones. For instance, a re-release of *The Adventures of Sherlock Holmes* as an eBook could include added features like a hyperlinked table of contents or annotations explaining Victorian-era references. These interactive enhancements make classic stories more accessible, particularly to younger readers or those new to the material. The portability of eBooks also caters to a fast-paced audience looking for convenience, allowing classics to fit seamlessly into their daily lives.

Print editions, on the other hand, hold a special place for collectors and traditionalists. There's something irreplaceable about holding a physical book, especially when it has been deliberately curated. A deluxe, illustrated version of *Pride and Prejudice* with elegant typography and custom artwork, for example, would appeal to readers seeking a tactile, collectible item. Formats like print-on-demand make such projects more feasible for independent creators, allowing you to strike a balance between quality and affordability. Print editions also allow you to explore niches like coffee table books or deluxe boxed sets, which can stand out as high-end offerings in a crowded market.

Audiobooks, meanwhile, tap into an entirely different consumer base. With people increasingly relying on audio content during their commutes or while multitasking, audiobooks offer unparalleled accessibility. Imagine transforming Herman Melville's *Moby-Dick* into an audiobook narrated by a seasoned voice artist whose cadence reflects the dramatic ebb and flow of the sea. This could provide an immersive experience that translates the epic narrative into something modern listeners can absorb and enjoy effortlessly. Audiobooks also present opportunities for dramatization, with multiple voice actors, music, and sound effects adding a cinematic layer to the storytelling, bringing certain works to life in unprecedented ways.

Emerging technologies like augmented reality (AR) offer powerful mechanisms to bring historical and literary classics into the future. For instance, AR-enhanced editions of Jules Verne's *Twenty Thousand Leagues Under the Sea* could feature interactive maps of Captain Nemo's voyage or 3D displays of underwater creatures as readers progress through the story. This type of innovation not only captivates younger and tech-savvy audiences but also pioneers a space where literature and technology merge seamlessly. Similarly, serialized storytelling platforms like Kindle Vella open doors for reimagining classic works as bite-sized episodic adventures, allowing creators to break down dense narratives into more digestible pieces and build suspense among readers over time.

More than anything, selecting the right format involves understanding your target audience. Fans of gothic literature might eagerly consume a new audiobook series of Edgar Allan Poe's tales if it integrates eerie soundscapes to amplify dread. Conversely, fans of children's literature would appreciate colorful, playful print versions of *Aesop's Fables*, with illustrations tailored to contemporary tastes. Staying attuned to market trends, such as the rising popularity of certain genres or new content consumption habits, can significantly influence which format will most effectively bridge the gap between timeless works and today's audience demands.

This chapter not only explores these formats in greater depth but also equips you with practical strategies for selecting and implementing them. By navigating the challenges of execution, whether it's mastering eBook formatting, ensuring print quality standards, or designing AR features, you'll find yourself prepared to bring public domain treasures to life. Whether aiming for functional accessibility or immersive innovation, the choices you make about format will ultimately dictate how successfully your project engages and profits from its audience.

Choosing the Right Format

The first step in repackaging public domain content is deciding on the most effective medium to bring the work to life. The right format can elevate classic material, making it widely accessible, relevant, and engaging for new audiences. This choice is not arbitrary; it requires careful consideration of the content's theme, the preferences of the target audience, and the strengths of each format. Some works demand the tactile elegance of print, others thrive as digital innovations, and a select few find their full potential as immersive audio experiences. Each medium offers unique benefits, and aligning the format with audience expectations can significantly impact how the work is perceived.

Print books are a classic choice and remain a favorite among collectors and traditional readers. For works like a Victorian-era etiquette guide, the physical format itself can enhance the theme, transforming the book into a chic coffee table piece. Specialty elements such as embossed covers, premium paper stock, or gilded edges add a sense of luxury and nostalgia that digital formats simply cannot replicate. Print-on-demand services provided by platforms like Amazon KDP or Lulu have opened the door to creators who want to produce high-quality physical editions without the financial burden of large print runs or storage. A thoughtfully designed print book, from its layout to its binding, can elevate the user experience, making the work feel exclusive and memorable. Recent successes in this arena include re-releases of Jane Austen novels as collector's editions featuring custom illustrations and introductions, which turned timeless classics into modern treasures.

Digital formats, especially eBooks, continue to grow in popularity due to their convenience and accessibility. The flexibility of an eBook allows creators to make significant enhancements, such as hyperlinked tables of contents, interactive glossaries, and embedded visuals that breathe new life into existing texts. For instance, updating a scientific masterpiece like *On the Origin of Species* with annotations and modern illustrations can help readers understand its historical and scientific contributions while making it more engaging. Additionally, eBooks lend themselves to modular, thematic compilations; a creator could group multiple works by Edgar Allan Poe, categorizing them into horror, mystery, and poetry collections, all packed into a single, easily navigable digital format. Because revisions are quick and cost-effective, digital formats allow creators to experiment with fresh ideas and respond rapidly to changing trends.

Audiobooks, on the other hand, tap into a growing segment of the market looking for mobility and immersion. They remove the barrier of sustained focus, enabling audiences to enjoy literature during commutes, workouts, or quiet evenings at home. Narration quality transforms text into theater, capturing intonation, emotion, and pace in ways that a printed page cannot. A suspenseful work like Edgar Allan Poe's short stories could become an entirely new experience when performed by voice artists capable of injecting chills into the pauses and punctuation. Beyond the narration itself, audiobooks allow for creative enhancements such as sound effects and music. For example, reimagining Mary Shelley's *Frankenstein* with eerie soundscapes and a dynamic narration could resonate deeply with fans of gothic storytelling while attracting new listeners curious about an immersive audio experience. Platforms such as Audible and ACX provide tools for independent creators to venture into audiobook production, making the process more accessible than ever.

Choosing the appropriate format also involves matching it to the expectations and natural habits of the intended audience. Younger readers might gravitate toward interactive eBooks or gamified versions of classic fairy tales, where they can explore vivid illustrations or notes tailored to a modern perspective. Similarly, audiobooks with immersive narration or a theatrical production may appeal to busy professionals seeking to reconnect with the classics in moments otherwise lost to the hectic pace of modern life. To craft a compelling offering, creators must analyze how each format enriches the material and provides the best possible experience for the audience.

Quality is another defining factor in this decision-making process. A print book with exquisite typography and layouts, an eBook with seamless navigation across devices, or an audiobook featuring a captivating voice artist all meet a baseline of professional standards that every consumer expects. Neglecting these details can diminish a work's appeal, regardless of its quality or historical relevance. For print projects, elements such as durable bindings, custom artwork, and professional cover design demonstrate a commitment to excellence. By comparison, for digital formats, compatibility with e-reader platforms and responsive design are key factors in ensuring a smooth user experience.

Ultimately, the medium you select helps to define your repackaged work, influencing how audiences experience it and where they interact with it. Print editions maintain their charm through high-quality production and niche appeal, while digital formats present cost-effective, versatile ways for reaching audiences worldwide. Audiobooks engage new listeners by combining storytelling artistry with modern streaming accessibility. The fusion of content, quality, and presentation aligned with a chosen format has the power to revive forgotten gems, allowing them to stand out amid contemporary offerings and extend their legacy into the future.

Delving Into Audiobook Production

Audiobooks have evolved into one of the most dynamic ways to consume literature, making them an excellent choice for repackaging public domain works. Their popularity stems from their convenience and accessibility, catering to listeners during commutes, chores, or downtime. By converting a classic text into an audio format, you're not only breathing new life into the work but also reaching an audience that might never have considered engaging with it in written form. Audiobooks have the power to transform static prose into a living, breathing performance, resonating with contemporary tastes and listening habits.

Platforms like ACX (Audiobook Creation Exchange) have democratized the audiobook production process, enabling anyone—from independent creators to larger publishers—to produce and distribute audiobooks with relative ease. ACX connects creators with professional narrators, known as audiobook producers, or provides tools for uploading high-quality, self-produced content. Other platforms, such as Findaway Voices, also offer valuable resources, including global distribution channels that help creators access wider markets.

For budget-conscious creators, recording the narration themselves is a viable option, though it does require some investment in time and equipment. Key elements for self-production include a high-quality USB microphone, noise-canceling headphones, and acoustic treatments like foam panels to minimize background noise. Free or low-cost software such as Audacity or GarageBand can handle recording and editing tasks effectively, while tools like iZotope RX can help clean up audio imperfections. However, self-narration isn't just about reading aloud; it demands skillful pacing, intonation, and emotional delivery to keep listeners engaged. For instance, reading H.G. Wells's *The Time Machine* may require varying the tone to capture both the protagonist's awe and trepidation while exploring unknown realms, ensuring the listener feels immersed in the unfolding adventure.

If the text calls for a more nuanced or theatrical performance, hiring a professional voice artist often delivers superior results. Skilled narrators can add layers of depth and emotion, bringing complex characters or dramatic scenes vividly to life. Audiobooks laden with dialogue or intricate prose especially benefit from voice actors who can differentiate characters and convey subtle context through tone and pacing. A captivating retelling of *Little Women*, for example, could feature a narrator who balances the warmth and humor of Jo March's youth with the poignancy of the sisters' challenges, creating an intimate connection with the audience.

For creators with a larger creative vision, incorporating sound effects and original music can elevate an audiobook from a simple reading to an immersive auditory experience. Consider Mary Shelley's *Frankenstein*, where the addition of thunderous storm effects and a foreboding orchestral score could heighten tension and highlight the gothic horror of the story. Dramatized adaptations, with multiple narrators voicing different characters, can further enrich the storytelling, turning classic narratives into cinematic experiences. Recent dramatized productions of *Dracula*, for instance, have attracted significant acclaim for their use of atmospheric sound design, transporting listeners into the eerie world of Transylvanian castles and London fog.

Creatively enriching audiobooks, however, does come with potential challenges. High-quality production requires reliable recording equipment, soundproof environments, and skilled editing, all of which can quickly escalate costs. For creators working on a limited budget, exploring partnerships or revenue-sharing agreements with talented freelance narrators can provide an alternative. Some narrators, particularly those building their portfolios, may agree to a royalty-share model through platforms like ACX, reducing upfront expenses. For creators short on technical expertise, collaborating with audio engineers through marketplaces such as Fiverr or Voices can ensure professional standards are met without exceeding reasonable budgets.

Another challenge lies in maintaining listener engagement, particularly with dense or lengthy texts. Breaking long works into digestible chapters or structuring the audiobook around thematic sections can enhance the listening experience. For example, a comprehensive reading of *The Iliad* might segment the epic into key battles or character arcs, allowing listeners to pause and reflect without losing track of the narrative. Dynamic pacing and voice modulation also play a huge role in holding audience attention, emphasizing the importance of selecting a narrator with the right skill set for your particular work.

One of the most rewarding aspects of audiobook production is its ability to introduce timeless stories to entirely new audiences. Listeners who might shy away from dense or archaic language in written form can find themselves captivated by a skillfully narrated version of the same text. Audiobooks offer a fresh avenue for engagement, transforming the reading experience into something portable, vibrant, and deeply personal. They also fit seamlessly along the curve of modern consumption habits, where audio content—from podcasts to audio drama—is a preferred medium for many.

Ultimately, audiobooks provide creators with an unparalleled opportunity to reimagine public domain works, making them accessible and appealing to contemporary audiences. Whether it's a dramatized version of Shakespeare's plays, a straightforward reading of a philosophical treatise, or an immersive production complete with soundscapes and music, the possibilities are boundless. By investing time in high-quality execution and leveraging creative enhancements, creators can ensure their audiobooks stand out as compelling interpretations of timeless classics.

Exploring Emerging Formats

The rapid advancement of technology has revolutionized the way we interact with literature, opening doors to formats that were once unimaginable. Emerging formats such as interactive eBooks, serialized platforms, and augmented reality (AR) experiences are transforming how people engage with stories and ideas. These innovations cater particularly to younger, tech-savvy audiences who crave interactivity, immediacy, and a sense of connection in their reading experiences. By tapping into these cutting-edge mediums, creators have the potential to reintroduce public domain works in ways that are both innovative and accessible.

Interactive eBooks are perhaps the most natural evolution of traditional text, offering readers the opportunity to engage with literature on a deeper level. These digital books go far beyond static words on a screen, incorporating features such as annotations, embedded videos, mini-games, and hyperlinks that enhance comprehension and enjoyment. For example, an interactive edition of Homer's *The Odyssey* could feature clickable maps charting Odysseus's epic voyage, providing historical context and visualizing the geographical scope of the story. Educational markets, in particular, are increasingly receptive to interactive content that enhances learning, making this format an excellent choice for classic texts used in schools. A collection of Aesop's fables, for instance, could add quizzes, glossaries, and simple animations to help young readers grasp the moral lessons behind each tale.

The customizability of interactive eBooks doesn't just stop at educational uses. Classics like *The Divine Comedy* could include 3D visuals of Dante's vivid depictions of Hell, Purgatory, and Paradise, or footnotes that expand on the symbolism and historical references within the text. Readers could deepen their enjoyment and understanding by exploring these additional layers of content, making the format an ideal bridge between timeless literature and modern entertainment.

Serialized platforms such as Kindle Vella have also emerged as an exciting way to repackage long and complex works. Unlike traditional eBooks, serialized content is released in episodic installments, allowing readers to consume stories in digestible segments. This approach is ideal for adapting monumental texts like Tolstoy's *War and Peace*. Rather than presenting the entire novel at once, creators could focus on individual storylines or character arcs within self-contained episodes. For example, Natasha's romantic turmoil or Pierre's philosophical dilemmas could play out over several entries, encouraging readers to eagerly anticipate the next installment. Serialized storytelling invites creators to experiment with nonlinear narratives or alternate viewpoints, breathing new life into well-loved classics while preserving their core essence.

Serialization also lends itself well to modern attention spans and reading habits, attracting audiences who prefer to engage with content during brief breaks in their day. Additionally, the episodic nature of these platforms builds suspense, turning even familiar stories into compelling cliffhanger experiences. Creators can use reader feedback to guide the progression of future episodes, making serialized platforms a dynamic space for collaborative storytelling and fostering an ongoing engagement with the audience.

Perhaps the most revolutionary of the emerging formats is augmented reality, which has the potential to completely transform the experience of consuming literature. By blending the physical and digital worlds, AR creates immersive environments that allow users to interact with a narrative in unparalleled ways. Imagine reading Emily Dickinson's poetry while walking through a digital recreation of her Amherst garden, complete with butterflies fluttering on AR glasses or phone screens in response to her words. Such an experience would do more than recreate her verses; it would envelop the reader in the emotions and atmosphere that inspired them.

AR offers particularly compelling applications for visually rich texts or works grounded in fantastical settings. For a title like Jules Verne's *Journey to the Center of the Earth*, readers could use AR to explore interactive maps of subterranean worlds or examine digitally-rendered creatures described in the text. Similarly, Shakespeare's plays could combine AR with theater, allowing users to view performances overlaid on real-world backdrops, such as a holographic Romeo and Juliet acting out the famous balcony scene in a local park. These experiences turn passive reading into active discovery, capturing the imagination and grounding timeless works in modern technology.

While these emerging formats open a world of new creative possibilities, they also come with unique challenges. Interactive eBooks, for instance, require technical expertise to integrate features like animations or hyperlinks seamlessly. For small-scale creators, outsourcing these tasks to professionals or learning user-friendly tools like Kotobee or Sigil can help overcome the initial hurdles. Serialized platforms demand consistent updates and careful plotting to sustain reader interest, requiring creators to balance commitment and flexibility. Additionally, AR experiences often involve substantial development costs and resources, potentially limiting accessibility for independent producers. However, partnerships with tech developers or leveraging pre-existing tools such as Unity or ARKit can make these ambitious projects more feasible.

At their core, these formats provide an opportunity to engage modern audiences in ways that go beyond the written word. Interactive eBooks turn static reading into a multimedia experience, serialized platforms adapt long works for today's fast-paced lifestyles, and AR brings stories to life in ways that make them feel novel and immediate. By harnessing the potential of these technologies, creators can reimagine public domain works not as relics of the past but as vibrant, evolving pieces of art capable of captivating audiences for years to come.

Addressing Challenges and Offering Solutions

Adapting public domain content into modern formats presents exciting opportunities, but the process can also bring a unique set of challenges. From technical hurdles in audio production to the precision required for print formatting or the complexities of interactive media development, creators must approach each obstacle with thoughtful planning and strategic solutions. By leveraging affordable tools, forming collaborative partnerships, and focusing on quality, these challenges can transform into opportunities for innovation and creativity.

Navigating Audiobook Production Costs and Quality

Audiobook production requires meticulous attention to sound quality and presentation, which can be daunting for creators new to
the medium. Hiring professional voice talent and audio editors often yields the highest-quality results but can carry significant costs.
For those with tighter budgets, partnering with emerging narrators
through platforms like ACX (Audiobook Creation Exchange) can
provide a cost-effective solution. Many narrators are open to revenue-sharing agreements, where rather than an upfront payment, they
receive a share of the audiobook's future profits. This arrangement
lowers financial risk while encouraging collaboration.

Creators who wish to narrate their own audiobooks need not invest in prohibitively expensive studio setups. Affordable USB micro-
phones, like the Blue Yeti or Audio-Technica AT2020, paired with
proper acoustic treatments such as foam panels or even DIY solutions
(e.g., recording in a closet or under a heavy blanket), can produce
surprisingly clean results. Free tools like Audacity or beginner-friendly
editing software like GarageBand allow creators to polish recordings
without hiring an outside editor. Additionally, online tutorials and
creator forums provide invaluable guidance on improving vocal delivery, editing techniques, and mastering sound files.

For creators aiming to stand out, adding atmospheric elements
such as background music, effects, or a multi-voice cast can elevate
the listening experience. While these elements require more time
and effort, options like pre-licensed sound libraries or collaborating
with composers on platforms like Fiverr can streamline the process.
Case studies like dramatized adaptations of *Dracula*, which combined
soundscapes with theatrical narration, demonstrate how relatively
low-cost additions can amplify audience engagement and make a work
feel fresh.

Tackling Print-On-Demand Challenges

Print-on-demand services offer an affordable way to create physical editions, but preparing polished files ready for printing can prove tricky. Formatting inconsistencies, like margins misaligned with bleed areas or blurry images, risk diminishing the professional appeal of a print book. Learning widely-used design tools such as Adobe InDesign or Canva can simplify the process of creating precise layouts that meet printing specifications. Resources like free templates or detailed publishing guides from platforms like Amazon KDP and Lulu can also aid in avoiding common errors.

For authors with limited graphic design experience, outsourcing cover design and layout tasks to freelancers through platforms like Upwork or 99designs can be a worthwhile investment. A professionally designed book cover often plays a decisive role in reader interest, and hiring experts ensures the aesthetics align with the content's theme. Collaborative efforts like the reimagining of Jane Austen novels as collector's editions—with embossing, custom illustrations, and consistent layouts—have successfully revitalized those classics for modern buyers. Considering details such as paper quality, durable binding, and premium finishes can similarly elevate smaller-scale print projects.

Print creators can also overcome challenges by tapping into the power of community resources. Joining writing or publishing groups, whether locally or online, fosters access to shared tools, expertise, and feedback that can save both time and money. Many creators find that community collaboration turns adversities like formatting difficulties into opportunities for fresh ideas and creative input from peers.

Overcoming Technical Barriers in Interactive and AR Media

Formats like interactive eBooks or augmented reality experiences are on the cutting edge of literary innovation but require advanced technical resources to execute effectively. Digital interactivity, such as clickable annotations, quizzes, or embedded multimedia, demands tailored programming skills or specialized software. Tools like Kotobee, iBooks Author, or Sigil simplify the creation of interactive eBooks, allowing creators to add features like audio clips or explanatory pop-ups without hiring a developer.

For augmented reality (AR) projects, digital landscapes and interactive experiences often require collaboration with skilled AR designers or 3D modelers. Platforms such as Unity or ARKit enable creators to build immersive content, but their learning curve can frustrate first-time developers. Forming partnerships with tech specialists can solve these challenges while fostering a team approach. Alternatively, some creators explore prototype-like solutions with simpler tools, focusing on smaller-scale, interactive elements.

Creators can seek funding for AR or interactive projects through crowdfunding platforms. Campaigns that showcase a clear creative concept often resonate with audiences eager to explore next-generation literary experiences. For instance, the idea of wandering through a digitally rendered landscape while hearing Emily Dickinson's lines recited in real time could inspire public excitement and financial support.

Balancing Quality and Cost

Whatever the medium, maintaining quality while managing costs is key to producing adaptations that stand out in a competitive market. Setting priorities early in the creative process helps allocate resources effectively. For example, audiobooks might benefit most from professional narration, while a print book's success may hinge on a top-tier cover design.

Using free online educational content or enrolling in budget-friendly workshops can empower creators to handle tasks like sound editing, book formatting, or basic programming themselves. Many creators also benefit from peer feedback, whether by joining interactive forums or through beta testing among trusted networks.

Despite the steep initial learning curves associated with some formats, innovative tools and collaborative opportunities mean creators today face fewer barriers than ever before. By exploring cost-effective solutions, leaning on creative communities, and maintaining a commitment to quality, creators can overcome production challenges and ensure their work resonates with modern audiences. This balance of practicality and artistry not only revitalizes public domain content but also allows it to thrive in fresh, engaging formats for years to come.

Building an Engaging Presentation

When it comes to making public domain content resonate with today's audiences, presentation is everything. Whether it's a physical book, a digital download, or an immersive experience, effective presentation has the power to set your work apart and capture attention. By focusing on visual design, marketing narratives, and audience engagement, you can ensure your project leaves a memorable impression and compels consumers to explore it further.

The Power of Visual Design

Visual design is often the first point of contact between your audience and your work, making it a critical component of marketability. For physical books, a visually compelling cover is indispensable. The design should encapsulate the tone, themes, and core essence of the work while standing out among competing titles. For example, a modern edition of *Pride and Prejudice* could feature elegant, minimalist floral patterns to evoke its romantic themes, while a gothic work like *Frankenstein* might benefit from dark, atmospheric imagery with bold typography. Touches like embossed lettering or matte finishes can add sophistication, appealing to collectors and avid readers alike.

For digital content, the same principles apply, but the focus extends to thumbnails, banners, and promotional graphics designed for online platforms. A digital edition of *The Great Gatsby*, for instance, could use vibrant, jazz-inspired Art Deco motifs. Creators can drive engagement by incorporating animated elements into social media ads or trailers. A simple animation of rising steam or flickering candlelight, paired with key quotes from the text, might be enough to intrigue viewers and spark interest.

Crafting Marketing Narratives That Resonate

Beyond visuals, the narrative behind your project can play a vital role in building anticipation and creating a personal connection with your audience. Marketing narratives that share the story of your work's transformation—from rediscovery to its modern interpretation—not only humanize your project but also spark curiosity. For instance, documenting the repackaging of a public domain classic like *Moby-Dick* could highlight its historical significance while reimagining the text for today's audiences. Why is the story still important? How has this new edition made it accessible for modern readers? Sharing answers to these questions through blogs, video vignettes, or social media posts helps consumers feel invested in the project's creative vision.

A great example of using storytelling is the campaign for the 200th-anniversary reprint of Mary Shelley's *Frankenstein*. Publishers shared Shelley's remarkable history as a teenage author, the book's groundbreaking themes, and its influence across centuries. By using behind-the-scenes videos of artists designing the cover and editors discussing updated annotations, the campaign created a sense of discovery and excitement.

Podcasts, in particular, provide a unique platform for building marketing narratives. Starting a podcast to explore the background of the public domain work, the challenges faced during adaptation, or the personal inspiration behind the repackaging process allows audiences to connect with the project on a deeper level. Engaging episodes centering on themes like "Why *The Picture of Dorian Gray* is Still Relevant Today" or "Unpacking the History of Victorian Ghost Stories" can create enthusiasm while positioning the work within broader cultural conversations.

Engaging Audiences Through Social Media and Multimedia

Successful projects don't just rely on aesthetics and backstories; they actively engage with their audience. Social media platforms, especially visual-oriented ones like Instagram, Pinterest, and TikTok, are powerful tools for building excitement. Share visually striking snippets of your project, such as time-lapse videos of artists illustrating a new book cover or sneak peeks of your audiobook production process. Engaging polls, quizzes, or trivia based on the content of your public domain work can also spark interaction. For example, a social media post asking, "What classic hero embodies your personality?" paired with stylized visuals can draw in curious audiences.

Teasers and trailers are another valuable way to build engagement. A short promotional video for an audiobook adaptation of Edgar Allan Poe's *The Raven* might include eerie sound effects, excerpts of dramatic narration, and atmospheric visuals like fluttering ravens or mist-filled graveyards. Multimedia posts like these pique curiosity while conveying the mood and themes of the work.

Additionally, creators can leverage platforms like Kickstarter or Patreon to involve consumers in the creation process itself. Crowd-funding campaigns that offer behind-the-scenes content or early access rewards incentivize audiences to become part of the project's journey. Pledgers might receive exclusive updates, a "thank you" credit in the final product, or limited-edition merch based on the work. This sense of involvement strengthens connections between creators and their audience, fostering loyalty and word-of-mouth promotion.

Examples of Successful Presentations

Many recent campaigns have proven how innovative presentation can captivate consumers. The rebranding of Shakespeare's works by the UK-based publisher Vintage Classics offered an excellent example of how polished design and strategic marketing intersect. By pairing bold, modern colors with simple typography and promoting the series with striking visuals on social platforms, they reached both traditional readers and younger audiences seeking aesthetically pleasing bookshelf additions. Meanwhile, the audio-drama adaptations of *Dracula* and

Jane Eyre by Audible combined marketing trailers, influencer reviews, and interactive fan giveaways to generate buzz before release. Their cinematic approach to presentation proved irresistible for audiobook fans and newcomers alike.

By marrying stunning design, authentic storytelling, and strategic digital engagement, creators can ensure their repackaged public domain content isn't just another revival but a fresh, unmissable experience. Thoughtful presentation transforms classics into cultural moments, cementing their relevance for today's audiences while honoring their cherished legacies.

Transforming the Past Into New Frontiers

Repackaging public domain works is more than just an exercise in adaptation; it is an opportunity to breathe new life into classic stories and ideas, transforming them into experiences that resonate with contemporary audiences. The formats and mediums creators choose not only determine how these works are consumed but also how they connect emotionally and intellectually with modern readers, listeners, and viewers. By balancing authenticity with innovative creativity, timeless works can evolve to thrive in today's cultural and technological landscape.

Unlocking New Mediums for Familiar Stories

Innovative formats elevate how audiences experience classic literature, offering more ways to access and engage with beloved texts. A forgotten epic like *Beowulf*, for instance, can transcend its origins when adapted as an immersive audiobook featuring stirring narrations, atmospheric sound effects, and epic musical scores. By recreating the legendary battles and emotional conflicts in audio format, creators engage listeners who might have found the dense poetry of the original daunting. Beyond accessibility, this reimagining deepens audience immersion and enjoyment.

Interactive formats push the boundaries even further. Classics like *Alice's Adventures in Wonderland* could be adapted into interactive eBooks where readers choose their paths as they follow Alice's adventures through whimsical mini-games and Easter eggs that expand on Lewis Carroll's unique world. Similarly, serialized storytelling platforms can offer fragmented or episodic adaptations of novels like *Les Misérables*, allowing readers to digest stories piece by piece, mirroring modern binge consumption patterns. A serialized approach might retell Fantine's tragic chapters or Javert's pursuit of Jean Valjean in focused, emotional segments, keeping audiences coming back for more.

Balancing Authenticity With Creative Adaptations

Reinterpreting classic stories is a careful balancing act between honoring the original and infusing it with modern relevance. The essence of a work must be preserved, but innovative techniques can add layers of appeal for today's audiences. Consider Shakespeare's plays, which have found new life through creative adaptations such as *Romeo + Juliet* (Baz Luhrmann's 1996 film), where the classic script met a modern, visually striking aesthetic. Similarly, stage productions like *Hamilton* have successfully connected historical figures with younger audiences by blending traditional narratives with modern music and multicultural casting, proving the timelessness of great stories when reimagined skillfully.

This approach could extend to public domain works like *Jane Eyre*, where perspectives or interpretations untapped in the original could be explored. A graphic novel format, for example, might bring Charlotte Brontë's gothic themes to life for readers who gravitate toward visually driven storytelling. Pairing dramatic imagery with key passages strengthens the visceral connection to Jane's struggles and triumphs while retaining the story's core authenticity.

Collaborating for Innovation

Although reimagining classics presents challenges, these often serve as gateways to creative partnerships and technical solutions that result in extraordinary outcomes. Collaborations between writers, designers, developers, narrators, and historians ensure that each piece of the adaptation process reflects both technical quality and artistic vision. For example, augmented reality (AR) projects based on public domain poetry might pair literary scholars with digital artists to render AR experiences that express both the emotional tones and visual imagery of the verses.

One inspiring example of creative collaboration is the digital adaptation of *Paradise Lost* as an interactive 3D experience. By pairing technology and art, creators allowed users to "walk through" Hell and Heaven as envisioned by Milton. Each layer of this adaptation highlighted the collaboration required to lift a centuries-old work into a next-generation format. Crowdfunding campaigns offering early glimpses into such collaborations further amplify excitement and add to the story's resonance before it reaches audiences.

Ensuring Relevance Across Generations

To make public domain works impactful for the future, creators must understand and adapt to shifting audience behavior while staying true to the timeless themes embedded in these classics. Works like *Dracula* find relevance today through formats tailored to modern interests; for instance, dramatic audiobook adaptations with soundscapes and cliffhanger episodes draw in podcast enthusiasts. Even more experimental transformations, like reinterpreting *A Christmas Carol* as a virtual reality (VR) experience where users interact with Scrooge or his spectral visitors, bring something entirely new to traditions steeped in legacy.

The key lies in recognizing the universal truths these classics uphold. Themes like redemption, love, ambition, and morality resonate today as deeply as when they were first written. By aligning those truths with the preferences of modern consumers (e.g., audiophile culture, interactive storytelling, or serialized binge content), creators bridge the gap between historical texts and today's cultural interests.

The Potential for Growth

Investing effort into adapting classics meaningfully pays dividends beyond financial success. These transformations renew interest in literature that might otherwise fade into obscurity. They also open opportunities for cross-disciplinary learning and exploration, such as pairing classical works with technology-oriented skillsets like coding or animation.

Ultimately, through thoughtful planning, attention to presentation, and a willingness to explore emerging formats, creators hold the power to forge new frontiers. Whether it's exposing young readers to classics through gamification, immersing audiences in cinematic audiobooks, or fostering community around serialized narratives, reimagined public domain works can continue to inspire, educate, and entertain for years to come. This synergy between the timeless and the new ensures that classics remain culturally vital and profitable, preserving their legacies while heralding their next chapter in history.

Chapter Six

Publishing Your Public Domain Work

Publishing public domain content offers a remarkable opportunity to tap into a vast reservoir of timeless works and breathe new life into them for modern audiences. These literary treasures are not just pieces of history but a foundation for your creative and entrepreneurial ambitions. With millions of works already available in the public domain, the possibilities for reimagining, revitalizing, and repurposing them are virtually endless. Whether your goal is to build passive income streams, establish yourself as a publisher, or share meaningful content with the world, the public domain offers a pathway that bypasses the often daunting task of creating something entirely new from scratch.

However, turning these opportunities into tangible results isn't as simple as uploading a file and waiting for success to come your way. The world of publishing is filled with nuances, especially when dealing with public domain material. Essential decisions, such as choosing between print-on-demand and traditional publishing, can significantly influence your project's reach and profitability. Furthermore, each publishing platform has its own rules, guidelines, and expectations for handling public domain works, which often require a thoughtful approach to ensure compliance and maximize your chances of success.

This chapter is designed to demystify the publication process for public domain works. We will not only address the practical steps you need to take but also guide you through the strategic decisions that are critical to your success. From selecting the right publishing platform and perfecting your book formatting to navigating platform-specific rules and setting your work apart from other public domain offerings, this chapter provides a comprehensive roadmap tailored to your needs.

By the time you finish reading, you'll have the clarity and confidence to bring your revitalized public domain content to market effectively. Whether you're a first-time publisher or looking to expand your publishing efforts, this chapter equips you with the tools and strategies to transform public domain potential into measurable success. The road ahead is filled with opportunities, and with the right approach, you can turn these hidden treasures into lasting achievements that resonate with modern readers.

Understanding Your Publishing Options

When venturing into publishing public domain works, understanding the available publishing methods is crucial to achieving your goals. The method you choose will influence everything from your operating costs and creative control to the speed at which your book reaches readers. Selecting the right path requires a clear understanding of your objectives, available resources, and how much time and effort you're prepared to invest in the process. Two primary options dominate the publishing landscape today: Print-on-Demand (POD) and Traditional Publishing. Each one offers unique benefits and challenges, making it essential to weigh your choices carefully before moving forward.

Print-on-Demand (POD)

Print-on-demand platforms have revolutionized book publishing by offering an accessible, cost-efficient solution for creators. These platforms enable you to publish physical books without dealing with the logistical burdens of preprinting inventory or managing warehouse storage. Instead, books are printed and shipped only when a customer places an order, ensuring you never need to invest upfront in bulk printing.

One of the most significant strengths of POD is its low financial barrier to entry. Traditionally, authors had to print hundreds or even thousands of copies of their book to reduce costs per unit, which often limited publishing opportunities to those with substantial capital. POD eliminates this hurdle, making it an attractive option for independent publishers or those starting with smaller budgets. This model also provides the flexibility to update or revise your book whenever needed, as no copies are stored in advance.

Another advantage is the variety of built-in tools that POD platforms offer, which make the publishing process more straightforward. For instance, platforms like Amazon's Kindle Direct Publishing (KDP) provide user-friendly interfaces for uploading your manuscript, creating book covers, and formatting your layout. With these tools, even first-time publishers can produce professional-quality books without hiring external services.

However, while POD offers convenience, it comes with compromises. The printing costs are deducted from each sale, which means profit margins per unit are often slimmer than traditional methods. Additionally, while many POD platforms guarantee decent quality, you'll have less control over advanced customizations such as specialty paper types, intricate cover designs, or high-end binding. If your target audience values premium aesthetics—for example, collectors or high-end graphic book enthusiasts—the limitations of POD might require a careful workaround.

Despite these challenges, POD remains a go-to choice for most public domain publishers for its accessibility and ease of scaling. Beginner-friendly platforms like KDP or Lulu are ideal starting points due to their extensive distribution networks, which allow you to reach a global audience with minimal effort. For those ready for more advanced integrations, platforms like IngramSpark offer robust options for expanded distribution, including access to brick-and-mortar bookstores.

Traditional Publishing

For creators seeking a more conventional route, traditional publishing presents an alternate approach. Unlike POD, which gives you complete autonomy over the process, traditional publishing involves submitting your book proposal or manuscript to established publishing houses. If your pitch is accepted, the publisher typically assumes responsibility for production, distribution, and marketing. For many authors, traditional publishing is appealing due to the prestige, credibility, and support it offers. However, this route is far from easy for creators working with public domain material.

One of the primary obstacles is the selection process. Traditional publishers are often reluctant to invest in content that already exists in some form or has multiple competing versions on the market. Public domain works, by their nature, fall into this category. However, if your project significantly enhances the original material—for example, by adding unique illustrations, a modern commentary, or a fresh narrative perspective—it stands a better chance of capturing a publisher's interest. For instance, an annotated edition of a literary classic with engaging expert insights could appeal to an audience seeking deeper understanding, making it a more attractive proposition to publishers.

Traditional publishing may also be advantageous if you have an existing platform or connections in the industry. For seasoned authors or individuals with an engaged following, pitching a revitalized public domain work as part of a series or a brand can improve your chances of securing a deal. Similarly, traditional publishers often have the resources needed to place your book in physical bookstores or libraries, something that POD platforms typically struggle to achieve at scale.

That said, the traditional route demands significant sacrifices. You should be prepared to relinquish creative control as publishers often take ownership of critical decisions like design, branding, and pricing. Additionally, while publishers provide upfront funding for production, they take a more substantial cut of the profits in return. This can significantly limit your earnings, especially if your work experiences niche or moderate success rather than widespread appeal.

For those considering this path, an effective pitch is essential. Focus on communicating what makes your revitalized public domain work unique and why the timing is right for its re-release. Words like "fresh perspective," "modern appeal," or "innovative design" can persuade publishers that your version of the work is more than just a reproduction; it's a marketable product with distinct value.

Balancing Your Goals and Resources

Choosing between POD and traditional publishing ultimately depends on what you want to achieve and what you can commit to the process. If you're building a publishing portfolio, trying your hand at entrepreneurship, or working with limited resources, POD platforms offer the quickest and most practical way to get started. The flexibility, control, and low risk they provide are ideal for newcomers and independent creators alike.

On the other hand, if you're drawn to the prestige of working with a traditional publisher or are looking to elevate an extensively enhanced public domain project, investing time in crafting a compelling pitch might be the better option. Keep in mind that traditional publishing requires persistence, as rejections are common, even for high-potential projects.

Ultimately, the publishing option you choose should align with your broader vision. Consider the scale of your project, the audience you're targeting, and how comfortable you are taking on a more hands-on publishing role. The good news is that both methods allow you to make public domain content accessible to new generations of readers, preserving its legacy while opening up new opportunities for profit and creative expression. The key is to start with clarity and move forward with confidence, knowing you've selected the path that best supports your vision.

Self-Publishing on Amazon Kindle Direct Publishing (KDP)

Among the various self-publishing platforms available, Amazon Kindle Direct Publishing (KDP) stands out as one of the best choices for creators working with public domain material. It's a platform designed for ease of use, making it accessible to beginners, while offering robust tools to help you reach a global audience. Whether you're publishing an eBook, a paperback, or both, KDP provides a streamlined process to bring your revitalized public domain work to market. This section covers every step you need to follow, offering practical advice along the way to maximize your chances of success.

Setting Up Your Account

Before you can begin publishing on KDP, you'll need to set up an account. Fortunately, Amazon's interface is straightforward, guiding you through the process step by step.

Start by signing into your Amazon account or creating one if you're new to the platform. Once logged in, visit the KDP dashboard and begin setting up your profile. Here, you'll link your KDP account to your payment and tax information, ensuring you're prepared to receive royalties from sales. KDP pays directly to your bank account, so be sure to double-check all details for accuracy to avoid delays or issues.

It's also a good idea to familiarize yourself with Amazon's payment structure and royalty schedules at this stage. For example, Amazon typically pays royalties every month, approximately 60 days after the end of the month in which your sales were recorded. Understanding this timeline will help you plan your finances as you begin your publishing journey.

Formatting and Uploading Your Work

Once your account is ready, the next step is preparing your manuscript for upload. Professional formatting plays a crucial role in making your work look polished and appealing, encouraging readers to take your book seriously.

For eBooks, KDP accepts manuscript files in formats such as .docx or Kindle-friendly formats like .mobi. Use tools like Kindle Create, a free program provided by Amazon, to format your manuscript for optimal readability on Kindle devices. Kindle Create simplifies tasks like adding chapter headings, table of contents links, or enhanced visuals.

For print books, your manuscript should be in .PDF format to preserve the exact layout. For this, programs like Adobe Acrobat or Vellum are excellent options. Remember to use high-quality fonts and proper line spacing to give your book a professional feel. Double-check margins, as they must meet the specific requirements of KDP's print-on-demand service to ensure your physical book prints correctly.

Equally important is designing a cover that captures attention at a glance. Readers often judge books by their covers, so investing time or resources in this area pays off. You can use design tools like Canva for creating covers or hire a freelancer through platforms like Fiverr or Upwork for a more tailored, professional result. Make sure your cover meets KDP's size specifications for your chosen format, as improperly sized images can lead to processing delays.

When you're ready to upload, click the "Add eBook" or "Add Paperback" option on your KDP dashboard. Follow the prompts to upload your manuscript and cover, ensuring they meet Amazon's formatting guidelines. The system will alert you to any errors, so take the time to resolve these before proceeding.

Pricing and Publishing

KDP provides you with the flexibility to set your book's price and royalties, allowing you to tailor your strategy based on your goals. For eBooks, you can select a 35% royalty rate for books priced below $2.99 or above $9.99, or a 70% royalty rate for books priced within that range. Carefully consider the cost of your enhancements and the market demand when determining your price.

For physical books, calculate your profit margins by factoring in production costs, which vary depending on book length, dimensions, and color settings. KDP's pricing calculator tool can help you predict your earnings per sale at different price points. For instance, a black-and-white paperback will be significantly cheaper to produce than a full-color version, so think strategically about what best suits your audience and budget.

One specific requirement for publishing public domain works on KDP is demonstrating the text's public domain status. Clearly detail in the metadata section where the content originates from and what enhancements you've added to distinguish your version. This might include annotations, illustrations, or modern language updates. For example, if you're publishing an annotated version of "Pride and Prejudice," specify in the description how your version expands upon the original text through added context or analysis.

Once these details are complete, you can hit "Publish." Amazon typically reviews submissions within 72 hours, during which they verify both the content and its compliance with platform policies.

Practical Tips for Success

To get the most out of your KDP publishing experience, consider the following tips:

- **Proofread and Review Extensively:** Before submitting your work, triple-check for typos, formatting issues, or inconsistencies. Consider using editing software like Grammarly or hiring a proofreader to catch errors you may have missed.

- **Draft a Compelling Book Description:** Your book's description is one of the most powerful tools for grabbing the attention of potential buyers. Highlight what makes your version unique and why readers should choose it over others. Use persuasive, engaging language tailored to your target audience.

- **Optimize Keywords and Categories:** During the setup process, KDP allows you to assign keywords and categories to help readers find your book. Research high-traffic, relevant terms using tools like Publisher Rocket to fine-tune your choices.

- **Enroll in KDP Select (Optional):** If you're publishing an eBook, consider enrolling in KDP Select. This program allows your book to be included in Kindle Unlimited, Amazon's subscription-based reading service, which can increase exposure and, in turn, royalties.

- **Leverage Amazon Previews:** KDP's "Look Inside" feature allows readers to preview the first 10% of your book. Pay extra attention to crafting a strong opening that hooks readers, as this can significantly impact your conversion rate.

Self-publishing on KDP opens the door to limitless opportunities for public domain creators. The platform's ease of use, combined with its global reach, makes it an ideal choice for both newcomers and seasoned publishers. By following best practices and presenting a professional, distinctive product, you'll be well-positioned to find success in this thriving marketplace. With the right approach and careful preparation, you can turn your revitalized public domain work into a standout offering that captures the attention and appreciation of modern readers.

Navigating Platform-Specific Rules for Public Domain Content

Publishers of public domain material often need to adapt to the unique guidelines of different self-publishing platforms. These rules are in place to ensure quality and prevent the marketplace from becoming oversaturated with duplicate or low-value works. Awareness of these requirements is essential to a smooth publishing experience and reducing the chances of rejections or other issues. This section explores the policies of popular platforms like Amazon Kindle Direct Publishing (KDP), IngramSpark, Lulu, and Draft2Digital, offering insights to help you stay compliant while maximizing your book's potential reach.

Amazon KDP

Amazon KDP is one of the most accessible platforms for independent publishers, but it maintains specific rules for public domain content to discourage market oversaturation. While the platform is beginner-friendly, it enforces rigorous policies to differentiate high-value modifications from straightforward reproductions.

To publish public domain works on KDP, you must fulfill the following requirements:

- **Prove Copyright Expiry:** KDP requires you to confirm and document that the source material's copyright has expired or that it belongs to the public domain. This involves specifying the original publication date and legal status in your book's metadata. A helpful note in your book description can reinforce this, such as "This book is based on material from [Title] originally published in [Year], which is in the public domain according to U.S. copyright law."

- **Demonstrate Value Additions:** Amazon discourages multiple identical reprints of public domain works. To stand out and gain approval, you'll need to make significant contributions to the original material. Examples of acceptable modifications include adding unique illustrations, detailed annotations, a new introduction or foreword, or contextual commentary that enhances the reader's experience. For instance, if you're republishing a work like "The Art of War," crafting a chapter-by-chapter analysis or placing the text in a modern context can make your version unique.

Failing to add meaningful enhancements can lead to rejections or limited visibility in Amazon's marketplace. If competitors are already selling well-established versions of the same public domain title, think creatively about what extra value your edition can offer.

IngramSpark

Unlike Amazon KDP, which is known primarily for its digital reach, IngramSpark excels in print distribution. Books published through this platform can gain access to libraries, independent bookstores, and even chain retailers like Barnes & Noble. However, this wider reach comes with more stringent requirements for public domain content.

- **Setup Costs and Formatting Standards:** Unlike KDP, which is free to use, publishing through IngramSpark comes with setup fees. Publishers need to be prepared to pay for these upfront costs as well as accommodate more advanced formatting standards. This higher standard often means investing in professional assistance for typesetting and layout, especially for print versions.

- **Detailed Enhancement Requirements:** Similar to Amazon, IngramSpark requires proof of significant modifications to public domain works. To avoid rejection, explicitly highlight your value additions in your book's description and metadata. Given its focus on print sales, enhancements like redesigned covers, typographical upgrades, or entirely reimagined visual presentations (e.g., a graphic novel adaptation) often perform well on this platform. For example, transforming "The Time Machine" into a beautifully illustrated edition with modern designs could appeal to collectors and draw new readers.

If you aspire to place your book on library shelves or bookstore displays, emphasizing its unique selling points tailored to these audiences is crucial. This could include mentioning academic relevance, educational utility, or aesthetic appeal in your pitch to distributors.

Lulu

Lulu is an excellent platform for creating niche publications and offers more creative freedom for public domain content. It emphasizes small-scale printing with options for hardcover books, spiral-bound editions, and other specialty formats that might appeal to unique markets.

- **Flexibility in Enhancements:** Lulu tends to be less rigid in its demands for value additions compared to Amazon or IngramSpark. However, to attract readers and avoid appearing redundant, adding unique elements to public domain texts is still important. Customizations such as luxurious binding, handwritten-style font choices, or even personalized editions targeting specific demographics (e.g., educators or historians) can set your book apart.

- **Distribution Options:** Lulu's distribution network includes the Lulu bookstore, which serves niche audiences, and optional access to extended channels like Amazon or Barnes & Noble. However, inclusion in these channels often requires the same transparency regarding copyright status and added value contributions as seen on KDP and IngramSpark.

Draft2Digital

Draft2Digital specializes in wide digital distribution, making it a valuable tool for eBook publishers seeking to expand beyond Amazon. It channels your work to storefronts like Apple Books, Barnes & Noble's Nook, and Kobo, as well as international markets.

- **Public Domain Documentation:** Similar to other platforms, you must confirm the copyright-free status of your work and outline the specific contributions you've made. Draft2Digital may request additional information about your modifications, so be prepared to defend the originality and relevance of your enhancements.

- **Formatting Considerations:** Draft2Digital provides free formatting tools to help make your eBook look professional. However, investing time or resources into quality formatting is always recommended for public domain publishing, as it will help distinguish your version from basic reprints.

- **Niche Distribution Appeal:** While Draft2Digital lacks the physical print focus of platforms like Lulu or IngramSpark, its wide digital reach allows you to target niche or underserved markets effectively. For example, an eBook edition of "The Federalist Papers" with thoughtful modern analysis aimed at students or political enthusiasts could perform well across its distribution channels.

Practical Tips for Navigating Platform Requirements

To ensure compliance and avoid common pitfalls on any publishing platform, keep the following principles in mind:

- **Be Transparent:** Clearly outline the origin of your public domain material and any modifications made. Platforms appreciate honesty and may deny approval if transparency is lacking or enhancements are unclear.

- **Focus on Quality:** Simple reprints of public domain texts are likely to go unnoticed or be rejected. Invest in enhancing the content or presentation, such as updated formatting, exclusive illustrations, or fresh commentary.

- **Tailor by Platform:** Customize your approach based on each platform's audience and strengths. For example, prioritize visual appeal for Lulu's niche print market but emphasize thorough digital formatting for Draft2Digital's eBook network.

- **Stay Updated:** Guidelines and policies change over time. Regularly revisit the publishing rules of your chosen platforms to ensure ongoing compliance with their standards.

By understanding and working within platform-specific rules, you can turn the potential pitfalls of public domain publishing into opportunities for success. Each platform offers unique strengths, and with careful planning and attention to detail, you can position your revitalized works to thrive in a competitive market.

Tips for Ensuring a Smooth Publishing Process

Embarking on the publishing process for a public domain work can be both exciting and complex. Successfully transforming a timeless piece into something that resonates with modern audiences involves making thoughtful decisions at every step. By proactively addressing critical aspects of the publishing process, you can avoid common mistakes, ensure compliance, and ultimately create a product that stands out in a competitive market.

Verifying the public domain status of your chosen work is an essential first step that reduces the risk of future complications. Thorough research into copyright laws and regulations will give you confidence in the legitimacy of your project. Trusted resources such as Project Gutenberg can help you identify works that are safely in the public domain, while the U.S. Copyright Office's databases offer official documentation to confirm the status of older texts. Conducting this research early saves you valuable time and shields your publishing efforts from potential legal challenges.

Investing in professional-grade tools is another critical component of the process. Software like Scrivener simplifies the writing and organizational stages of your project, allowing you to handle everything from outlining sections to completing final edits in one intuitive interface. For formatting and layout, programs like Vellum are invaluable. They help create clean, professional templates for both digital and print editions, ensuring your book meets the technical requirements of various publishing platforms. While these tools may have a learning curve or upfront cost, they dramatically reduce errors and present your book in the best possible light to readers.

One of the most important steps in publishing public domain content is clearly listing the enhancements you've made to the original work. Platforms such as Amazon KDP, which host countless public domain titles, prioritize projects that offer unique value. This might involve modernizing outdated language while retaining the tone of the original text, or adding visual interest through custom illustrations. Contextual elements, like new commentary or a foreword discussing the text's relevance today, can also elevate your version above others. Highlight these enhancements prominently in your book description and metadata. A well-written summary that explains your value-adds assures readers and platforms alike that your version stands apart from simple reproductions.

Publishing a public domain work successfully is more than submitting your manuscript and hoping for sales. Establishing and executing a structured publishing plan greatly increases your book's appeal and reach. Pre-launch preparation is crucial in this process. Treat your book like any other product release; start by creating a marketing strategy that includes generating buzz on social media and introducing your work to online communities that align with its theme or genre. Share teasers of your enhancements, such as a snippet of your new introduction or a preview of an illustration. Email lists can be particularly effective for reaching an engaged audience. Sending updates to readers who are already interested in your project helps build excitement and ensures a strong launch.

Post-launch, your work doesn't stop. Ongoing updates are vital for maintaining relevance and remaining competitive. Pay attention to the feedback you receive in reviews and comments from readers. This feedback often contains valuable insights, such as suggestions for additional content or corrections for minor errors. By addressing these critiques and releasing updated editions when necessary, you show readers that you value their input and are committed to delivering quality. Regular updates also help your work stay active in algorithms on platforms, increasing its visibility.

Expanding your format options is another way to maximize your book's impact. After successfully launching an eBook version, consider introducing your work in other formats like print or audiobook. Each format caters to a different segment of readers, allowing you to broaden your audience. With tools like ACX, producing an audiobook version is more accessible than many publishers realize. A talented narrator can bring your book to life in a way that appeals to listeners who prefer audio to text. Similarly, offering a physical edition through print-on-demand platforms opens opportunities to reach collectors and readers who want to experience your work in tangible form.

Navigating the publishing process for a public domain work requires careful attention to detail and a commitment to quality. By verifying copyright status, using the right tools, and clearly showcasing your enhancements, you ensure a smooth start. Coupling that with strategic marketing, active updates, and format diversification will keep your book fresh and competitive in the long term. Through deliberate effort and a focus on professionalism, you can take a timeless classic and transform it into a work that resonates with today's readers.

Closing Thoughts on Publishing Public Domain Works

Publishing public domain works is more than just a business venture; it's a unique opportunity to breathe new life into stories, ideas, and knowledge that have stood the test of time. It allows you to fuse your creativity with entrepreneurial skills, resulting in a project that not only connects with modern audiences but also preserves and celebrates literary heritage. This process asks a lot of you as a creator. It challenges you to think like an editor, designer, marketer, and publisher all at once, but it also gives back in rewarding ways.

The key to success lies in taking a methodical and detail-oriented approach. From researching copyright status to selecting the right platform, crafting thoughtful enhancements, and offering a polished product, every step matters. These small choices collectively determine whether your revitalized work fades into obscurity or becomes a standout addition to the marketplace. By closely adhering to platform-specific rules and staying open to feedback, you set yourself on a path not just to publish, but to thrive.

Yet this process isn't only about profits or sales figures; it's a contribution to the enduring legacy of classic works. By revisiting and reimagining these creations, you ensure that their wisdom, beauty, and cultural significance continue to inspire a new generation of readers. Whether you are updating language, adding illustrations, or creating insightful commentary, your efforts help these timeless pieces evolve, remaining relevant in an ever-changing world.

This mix of creativity, passion, and entrepreneurial drive is what makes publishing public domain works such a special endeavor. You're not just a creator but a curator, bridging the past and the present. With patience, persistence, and a commitment to excellence, you have the power to turn forgotten classics into meaningful modern contributions.

Every public domain project is an opportunity to reimagine a piece of history for today's readers. Take that first step, trust in your vision, and allow the process to unfold. By doing so, you're not only crafting books but creating connections across time, keeping the voices of the past alive and vibrant for the future. Now is your chance to be part of that story.

Chapter Seven

Creating a Brand Around Public Domain Content

When publishing public domain works, having a strong brand can mean the difference between being overlooked and becoming a trusted, go-to creator in your niche. A brand is more than just a memorable logo or a catchy tagline; it's the overall impression you leave on readers, encompassing the quality of your work, your values, and the personality of your business. Branding is about crafting a cohesive identity that represents who you are as a publisher, delivering clear and consistent messaging that resonates with your target audience. It's the promise of professionalism and quality that keeps readers coming back for more.

A strong brand builds trust by setting clear expectations. When readers see your beautifully designed covers or recognize your tone of voice in descriptions and announcements, they immediately associate your name with reliability and value. For instance, imagine a reader browsing through a crowded online marketplace filled with uninspired public domain reproductions. They're more likely to choose and recommend a publisher with a polished, cohesive brand identity that signals care and attention to detail, rather than a generic offering with little thought put into presentation.

Additionally, branding establishes your professional reputation as a curator and creator. You become more than just someone republishing free material; you're seen as an expert who selects, enhances, and contextualizes lost gems for today's audience. For example, a publisher specializing in revitalizing Victorian-era novels could develop a reputation for insightful forewords and stunning period-inspired illustrations. Such efforts elevate your work above the mass of unedited or unimproved versions, making your editions the audience's preferred choice.

Through intentional branding, you also cultivate an emotional connection with your readers. Maybe your brand reflects a passion for preserving timeless educational texts or reimagining forgotten tales with a modern flair. Communicating that mission through design, messaging, and engagement allows readers to align themselves with your vision. Over time, this creates loyalty not just for a single book but for your future releases, laying the foundation for a sustainable and respected publishing career in the public domain space.

Why Branding Matters for Public Domain Works

Public domain content offers a treasure trove of creative possibilities, but it also comes with unique challenges. One of the most significant is oversaturation. Because public domain works are freely available, the marketplace often becomes crowded with uninspired or low-effort reproductions. These unpolished editions can overwhelm readers, making it harder for them to distinguish between quality and mediocrity. Without a clear identifier that signals excellence, your work risks blending into the sea of generic offerings. This is where the power of a strong brand comes into play. By establishing a distinct and memorable identity, you can make your publications stand out as premium, go-to options, even in a saturated space. Readers are far more likely to choose an edition that reflects care and professionalism, particularly when they view your brand as a hallmark of added value.

A strong brand is like a signature of trust. It tells readers that your editions of public domain works go beyond the bare minimum. Perhaps your versions feature modern introductions, enhanced formatting, or striking new illustrations. Maybe you specialize in niche genres and consistently present them with deeper context. For instance, a reader interested in historical fiction might bypass generic print-on-demand books in favor of your well-curated editions, which include thoughtful commentary and stylish cover designs that match the era of the story. Over time, this attention to detail builds loyalty. A reader who loves one of your books will eagerly look forward to your next release, not just out of curiosity but because they associate your name with quality they can rely on.

Branding doesn't just help attract readers; it also helps forge long-term relationships with them. Loyal readers are more than one-time customers. They become advocates, recommending your books to others and following your publishing endeavors. This loyalty fosters repeat purchases, something especially significant in the public domain space where each new book can feel like part of a larger series or collection. For example, a publisher creating updated editions of classic philosophical texts could develop a following among students, academics, or hobbyists. Those readers would keep returning for new volumes, trusting the publisher's vision and expertise.

Your brand also enhances your professional reputation, which has ripple effects beyond your immediate audience. When you establish yourself as a creator who adds genuine value to public domain content, industry platforms and peers are more likely to take notice. Retailers may favor your books in search results due to higher sales, better reviews, and stronger presentation. Similarly, collaborations with illustrators or audiobook narrators become easier to secure when your brand is known for professionalism and consistency. Take the example of a publisher who modernizes children's classics. Their eye-catching adaptations might not only impress readers but also encourage retailers to feature them prominently in promotions, knowing the publisher delivers a superior product.

The benefits of branding extend even further. Your identity becomes a badge of credibility that resonates in the minds of both your audience and competitors. The consistent use of design elements, tone, and messaging helps you carve out a recognizable space in the market. While others struggle to differentiate themselves in a crowded field, your editions gain attention as curated, unique offerings. Whether through social media presence, engaging newsletters, or visually striking bookshelves, your brand evolves into a trusted name synonymous with value and creativity.

Ultimately, branding is essential for building meaningful connections with your audience and standing out in a competitive marketplace. It turns isolated purchases into long-term relationships, imprints trust in the minds of readers, and creates a framework in which your work is seen as both professional and essential. Investing in your brand ensures that your public domain offerings not only succeed in the present but become a lasting presence in a crowded and dynamic publishing world.

Developing a Professional and Recognizable Brand Identity

Crafting a powerful brand identity is a deliberate process that requires clarity and intention. At its core, your brand identity is the essence of who you are as a publisher and how you wish readers to perceive your work. The first step is identifying your mission and values, which serve as the foundation for every decision you make. Ask yourself why you're focusing on public domain works and what unique perspective you bring to this space. For example, are you passionate about reviving forgotten classics with modern commentary? Or do you specialize in beautifully illustrated editions for collectors? By understanding and articulating your mission, you ensure that your brand is not only authentic but also resonant with your audience. This clarity will guide your decisions, from the aesthetics of your book covers to the tone of your social media interactions.

One of the most crucial elements of brand identity is visual presentation. Your visual identity is often the first impression a reader will have of your work, so it must be professional, cohesive, and memorable. Start by defining a consistent style for your covers. If your niche involves historical fiction, you might opt for a vintage-inspired design with ornate typography. Alternatively, if you focus on revitalizing philosophical texts, a minimalist aesthetic with clean lines and neutral tones could better reflect your brand's intellectual appeal. Colors, fonts, and layout choices should work together to establish a recognizable look. Remember, your design choices should not just reflect the content of your books but should also communicate the overall personality of your brand.

Consistency extends beyond book covers to your website, social media platforms, and marketing materials. A visually uniform brand identity makes it easier for readers to recognize and differentiate you from competitors. For example, when viewers scroll through an online marketplace or their Instagram feed, your signature use of color palettes and typography can immediately make your editions stand out, even at a glance. If design isn't your strength, there are user-friendly platforms like Canva that provide customizable, professional templates. Alternatively, hiring a graphic designer may prove a worthwhile investment, especially if you're aiming to build a long-term, premium brand.

Equally critical is your tone of voice, which is the personality behind your words and messaging. Think of it as the way your brand "speaks" to readers. Are you aiming for approachability and warmth to resonate with casual readers? Or is your tone more formal and scholarly, tailored to academics or serious enthusiasts? For example, if you're republishing whimsical fairy tales, you might adopt a playful, engaging tone for your book descriptions and promotional posts. On the other hand, a brand focusing on important historical speeches might use a respectful, fact-driven tone that communicates authority. Regardless of your audience, consistency in your tone across all touchpoints—from product descriptions to newsletters or social media captions—is essential. A uniform voice builds authenticity and makes your brand feel like a trusted companion to your readers.

Consider, for instance, a publisher focusing on children's classics. Their visual identity might feature charming pastel covers with hand-drawn illustrations, while their tone of voice could be light-hearted, imaginative, and reassuring, appealing directly to parents and educators looking for timeless, high-quality editions. On the other hand, a brand specializing in gothic literature might employ dark, moody imagery combined with a more dramatic or mysterious tone in their marketing copy to captivate fans of the genre.

A professional and recognizable brand identity is what transforms a mere collection of books into a cohesive publishing imprint. It fosters familiarity, builds trust, and keeps your audience coming back for more. Through thoughtful visual design, consistent messaging, and an authentic voice, you can create a brand that leaves a lasting impression and carves a distinct space for your public domain works in a competitive marketplace.

Building an Audience That Trusts and Loves Your Approach

After developing your brand identity, the next critical step is creating a loyal audience that appreciates and trusts your work. Establishing meaningful connections with readers is about more than just selling books; it's about building relationships and fostering a sense of community around your publishing vision. To do this effectively, you need to combine authenticity, authority, and consistent engagement.

A foundational strategy for connecting with your audience is to establish yourself as a credible voice in your niche. Your expertise gives readers a reason to believe in your approach. If your focus is on republishing children's classics, for example, your audience will value your knowledge of the genre's history and cultural impact. Creating blog posts, articles, or video content that explores the origins and significance of beloved stories, or that highlights your unique contributions to revitalizing them, can make your vision stand out. Parents, educators, or literary enthusiasts will see you not just as a publisher but as a passionate curator who enhances their understanding and appreciation of timeless works.

Social media platforms serve as powerful tools for audience engagement, allowing you to reach readers where they are and share your creative process. Use these platforms to provide behind-the-scenes insights into your work. For instance, you could post videos or images showing how new illustrations are being developed for an upcoming release or demonstrate the care that goes into formatting and annotating your editions. Such intimate glimpses of your publishing process show dedication and craftsmanship, helping readers feel connected to the final product. You can also use interactive features like polls, Q&A sessions, and comment threads to create opportunities for participation. For instance, you might ask followers to vote on which classic they would love to see reimagined next, allowing them to feel directly involved in shaping your content.

Email marketing is another powerful way to engage on a more personal level. A regular newsletter can keep your audience updated on new releases, special projects, or exclusive discounts. But emails shouldn't just be about promoting new products. Share valuable insights, such as recommendations for similar classics, or include fun trivia about works you've revitalized. By offering your readers meaningful content, you turn your emails into something eagerly anticipated rather than something to delete.

Encouraging reviews and testimonials plays a huge role in building trust and demonstrating the quality of your work. Readers are far more likely to give a new publisher a chance if they see glowing reviews from others who were delighted with your editions. After a purchase, politely ask for feedback and make it easy for readers to leave reviews on platforms like Amazon or Goodreads. Don't forget to feature positive testimonials on your website and social media. For a more personal touch, showcase thank-you notes or reader photos, with permission, to illustrate the human connection that your work fosters.

Transparency and responsiveness are essential for building authentic relationships. Engage with your audience by answering questions, responding to comments, and acknowledging their feedback. If someone points out a mistake or suggests an improvement, own it and thank them for their input. Readers value approachable publishers who genuinely care about their opinions and experiences. Additionally, being transparent about your process can strengthen trust. For example, explaining why you chose to release a limited run of books or highlighting the challenges of reviving certain works can give readers a deeper appreciation for what goes into your craft.

Building an audience that loves and trusts your approach doesn't happen overnight, but the impact of sustained, thoughtful engagement can't be overstated. By combining online visibility with authenticity, authority, and genuine interaction, you'll create a solid foundation for reader relationships. These bonds, built on trust and shared enthusiasm, will drive loyalty, word-of-mouth promotion, and long-term success for your publishing endeavors. Whether through social media, email campaigns, or personalized interactions, your ability to connect with your audience will ultimately determine how deeply your work resonates and how far it can reach.

Managing Copyrights for New Additions and Enhancements

While public domain works are free for anyone to use, the creative enhancements you add to these works are your intellectual property. This means that elements like original illustrations, fresh editorial content, annotations, unique formatting, and any other significant contributions are eligible for copyright protection. Registering copyrights for these additions is a crucial step in safeguarding your work and ensuring that others cannot replicate your unique edition without permission or credit.

The first step in protecting your contributions is to officially register your copyrights. This process can be done through the U.S. Copyright Office or the equivalent government agency in your country. Registration provides a legal record of your intellectual property, equipping you with the necessary evidence and rights to pursue legal action in the event of infringement. It's not a complex process, but the protection it offers is invaluable. You'll typically need to submit a copy of your work, a completed application, and a small fee. Once registered, you'll receive a certificate of copyright that formally recognizes your ownership of the original additions.

Including a copyright notice in your publications is another important step. Though not legally required in many jurisdictions, prominently stating that your contributions are copyrighted helps deter potential infringers. For example, you could include a statement within your book or in its description, like this: "Original illustrations, formatting, and editorial content created by [Your Name/Publishing Brand] are protected under copyright law. The underlying work is public domain." This simple note reinforces both your ownership of enhancements and the transparency of your branding.

Transparency plays a vital role, both in building trust with your audience and ensuring compliance with publishing platforms. Online marketplaces like Amazon often have strict guidelines when it comes to the sale of public domain works. Clearly explaining in your book's product description which parts of the work are original and which stem from public domain content not only helps you meet these guidelines but also assures readers of the value you're adding. For example, you might include a line like, "This edition features newly commissioned illustrations, updated formatting for modern readers, and an in-depth introduction that contextualizes the original text."

Beyond compliance, being upfront about your contributions creates a sense of authenticity. Readers appreciate knowing that you've
put effort into offering something beyond a plain reprint. They want
to see how your expertise and creativity enhance their reading experience. Imagine a customer comparing two editions of a public
domain novel. One is a generic, unformatted reproduction, while the
other is your thoughtfully designed version with custom artwork and
insightful commentary. Transparency about these elements enhances
the perceived value of your brand and encourages purchases.

There's also a pragmatic side to documenting and registering your
additions. It ensures that others can't profit unfairly from your innovations. For instance, if another publisher tries to reuse your original
illustrations without permission, having registered copyrights gives
you the legal backing to file a cease-and-desist or pursue further action if necessary. This protection extends beyond direct copies; even
derivative works, like someone modifying your illustrations, may still
fall under your copyright depending on jurisdiction.

If you work with collaborators, such as illustrators or designers, it's
wise to have clear contracts in place that outline copyright ownership.
Decide upfront whether these collaborators retain rights to their work
or if you'll be purchasing exclusive ownership. These agreements make
it easier to establish legal boundaries and avoid disputes later on.

Ultimately, managing copyrights for your additions and enhancements is about valuing your work as much as your audience does. It
ensures that the time, creativity, and resources you invest in improving public domain texts are acknowledged and protected. By taking
proactive steps to secure your rights and being transparent about your
contributions, you establish yourself as a serious, trustworthy publisher in the public domain space, giving readers even more reason to
connect with and support your projects.

Turning Your Brand into a Legacy

A truly developed brand doesn't just represent the professional efforts you've put into revitalizing public domain works—it turns into a timeless legacy that reflects your creativity, dedication, and impact on the literary world. It evolves into something larger than a business name; it becomes a symbol of trust, quality, and innovation that resonates deeply with readers. Over time, it's this legacy that keeps your brand thriving not just for individual projects, but across generations of followers loyal to your unique approach.

The foundation of turning your brand into a legacy lies in consistently delivering value. When readers pick up your editions, they should always feel that they're receiving something exceptional. Whether it's thought-provoking commentary, meticulous formatting, or breathtaking new illustrations, these touches signal your commitment to excellence. Consistency builds trust, and trust fosters loyalty. Imagine a reader who tries one of your beautifully curated editions and enjoys it so much that they look for your name or brand every time they want to explore another classic. Gradually, your brand becomes synonymous with reliability and quality, earning recognition that extends far beyond your immediate audience.

Creativity is another powerful driver in building a lasting legacy. Public domain works may be widely accessible, but your original contributions breathe new life into these timeless texts, making them feel relevant for modern audiences. Your ability to reinterpret classics with a fresh perspective, or to present them in ways that surprise and delight, creates a distinct identity that sets you apart in a crowded market. For example, a brand specializing in steampunk-themed redesigns of literary classics might attract a niche but highly enthusiastic audience, while another focusing on educational, annotation-rich editions for classrooms might become a trusted resource for educators. By leaning into your creative strengths, you craft a bold vision that leaves a lasting impression.

The long-term benefits of building such a brand are undeniable. A loyal audience becomes the backbone of your success. These readers not only return for future releases but also act as ambassadors for your brand, recommending your work to friends, family, and others in their network. This kind of organic word-of-mouth promotion is invaluable, often surpassing the impact of advertising. Over time, the compounding effect of loyalty and referrals can elevate your brand from a small venture to an enduring name recognized by readers and even industry professionals.

Recognition amplifies your brand's reach and authority. As you consistently meet or exceed reader expectations, your reputation within your niche grows. This recognition can open new doors, like collaborations with other creators, invitations to literary events, or even opportunities for your editions to be featured in libraries, schools, or collector-focused publications. For example, a publisher known for crafting stunning, limited-edition collector's books might discover that their works are featured in gift guides or prestigious marketplaces, further solidifying their status as an industry leader.

Growth, while not immediate, is another key outcome of developing a legacy brand. A strong identity becomes the foundation for scaling your efforts. Once your brand is recognized as a hallmark of quality, expanding your catalog or exploring new niches becomes more fluid and impactful. Readers who trust your expertise in one genre, such as Victorian novels, may eagerly support your efforts when you branch into another, like early science fiction. Your trusted name acts as a bridge between creative experimentation and audience approval, giving you the flexibility to evolve while maintaining a loyal base.

Consider brands like The Folio Society, which has become a respected name in creating exquisite editions of classic works. Their commitment to high craftsmanship and unique design appeals to book collectors worldwide, ensuring their editions are not only desirable in the present but cherished as timeless pieces in the future. Similarly, by applying your own creative lens and maintaining professional consistency, you establish a reputation that will keep readers returning to your work for years to come.

Building a legacy brand isn't an overnight achievement; it's a long-term investment in your creative vision and your audience's trust. The process requires careful planning, patience, and a commitment to staying true to your mission. Whether you dream of becoming a widely recognized name in the literary world or simply want to share your passion for timeless works through a select but passionate audience, branding is the bridge that connects the present moment to a sustainable future.

Your brand legacy begins the moment you decide to pour your heart into each project, creating works that are not only valuable today but will continue to inspire readers for years to come. Over time, the combination of quality, creativity, and trust will ensure that your name endures as a symbol of excellence, marking its place in the stories both on the page and in the hearts of your readers.

Chapter Eight

Marketing and Selling Your Public Domain Book

Marketing and selling your public domain book is where the true transformation occurs. It's not enough to simply repackage and publish a timeless piece of literature; success lies in how effectively you can share its value with the world. This stage is the bridge between your creative efforts and financial reward, between your hard work and a reader discovering a book that speaks to them.

The key to profitable publishing isn't just in choosing the right book from the public domain, but in mastering how to position it in a marketplace brimming with options. Effective marketing strategies can breathe life into your book, driving interest, engagement, and ultimately, sales. It's how you turn obscurity into visibility and curiosity into commitment. Every campaign, every tactic, and every decision will play a role in ensuring that your book doesn't just sit on a digital shelf but actively reaches the hands of readers who can't wait to explore it.

At the heart of this effort is the connection you build with the right audience. Readers want to know why your interpretation or version of a public domain classic is worth their time and investment. They want to understand what sets it apart in a sea of books and how it resonates with their personal interests or aspirations. Marketing is as much about storytelling as it is about strategy. It's about sparking curiosity, solving problems, and evoking emotions that compel action.

The strategies outlined in this chapter will take you from simply having a book for sale to creating a buzz that drives its success. You'll learn how to build excitement around your publication, leverage the power of modern tools and platforms, and craft messages that resonate deeply with your target audience. A structured approach to marketing can elevate your book from being just another title to becoming a must-have item for devoted readers. Whether you're just starting out or looking to scale up your efforts, these insights will empower you to maximize visibility, build loyalty, and generate consistent profits. This is where your book finds its voice in today's crowded market, making your publishing venture both impactful and rewarding.

Building the Foundation for Success

Before you launch your marketing campaign, it's essential to ensure your book is properly packaged for success. A well-executed foundation sets the tone for how potential readers perceive your work and directly impacts their decision to purchase. Each element of your book's presentation must work together to communicate professionalism, value, and appeal.

A professional cover design is non-negotiable in today's competitive market. Readers often judge a book by its cover, and while the saying may be cliché, it couldn't be more accurate. Your cover is the first thing potential buyers see, and it needs to make an instant impact. Invest in a skilled graphic designer who understands not only aesthetics but also market trends and genre-specific expectations. For example, a modern take on classic literature might benefit from minimalistic, contemporary designs, while a historical piece may lean into vintage-inspired visuals. The right design won't just grab attention; it will signal the tone and content of the book, building an immediate connection with the reader.

The title of your book is equally important. A captivating title tells readers what to expect while sparking their curiosity. When reworking public domain material, carefully consider titles that highlight your book's unique angle. For instance, if you've added annotations or a fresh perspective to a classic text, emphasize that in the title. Avoid overly generic titles that could cause your book to blend in with the crowd. Instead, opt for something specific, engaging, and memorable. A strong title doesn't just label your work; it becomes part of the sales pitch.

Next, your book description is your opportunity to truly captivate potential readers. This is more than a summary of the content; it's a persuasive argument for why your book deserves a place in their collection. Use this space to tell a story about why your repurposed work matters now, in today's context. Highlight what makes it fresh and unique, whether it's updated features, improved usability, new illustrations, or editorial enhancements. Speak directly to your audience by addressing their interests or needs. For example, how does your version of the book solve a problem, provide clarity, or cater to an underserved niche?

Craft your headlines and hooks to immediately capture attention. The first few lines of your description should be bold and intriguing, compelling readers to continue. Write with sensory and emotional language that resonates, making the book feel relevant and essential to their lives.

Your product page plays a critical role as it serves as a virtual storefront for your book. Think of it as your best salesperson. Beyond the description, ensure that your product images, reviews, and layout create a seamless, professional impression. Include a preview of the book's content to give buyers a taste of what they'll experience. A professional touch, combined with attention to detail in every aspect of your book's presentation, will ensure you create a strong first impression that converts interest into sales.

Harnessing Advertising Strategies That Work

Paid ads can serve as a game-changing tool in driving readers to your book. By leveraging platforms like Amazon Ads and Facebook Ads, you can tap into highly targeted audiences based on their interests, purchasing habits, and demographics. These platforms allow you to amplify visibility and connect with the right readers, but success requires strategic planning and execution.

When using Amazon Ads, keywords are your greatest ally. Begin by conducting keyword research to identify phrases your target readers are already searching for. Study the top-performing books in your niche and analyze their keyword strategies. Which terms are they ranking for, and how can you tap into that search demand? Start by testing a mix of broader keywords that capture your genre (e.g., "classic literature" or "mystery novel") and more specific ones tailored to unique features of your book (e.g., "illustrated edition of timeless classics" or "annotated Sherlock Holmes"). Keep in mind that relevancy is key; the more targeted your keywords, the higher the likelihood that clicks convert into purchases.

Additionally, experiment with different types of Amazon ad campaigns, such as Sponsored Products, Sponsored Brands, and Lockscreen Ads for Kindle. Each offers distinct advantages, and their impact varies depending on your goals. For example, Sponsored Products are excellent for driving immediate visibility, while Sponsored Brands can boost your presence by showcasing multiple books if you have a series. Constantly monitor your campaign metrics, such as click-through rates, cost-per-click, and return on ad spend, to identify what's working. Small adjustments, like refining your keywords or switching up your ad copy, can significantly improve performance over time.

Facebook Ads, on the other hand, provide a unique opportunity to engage directly with reader communities. With Facebook's advanced targeting features, you can narrow your audience down to the finest details. Imagine you've republished a classic mystery novel. Facebook allows you to target users who are members of mystery book clubs, followers of popular detective authors, or members of niche groups centered around vintage crime stories. You can even layer these interests with demographic data, such as age, location, or education level, to get hyper-specific about whom your ad reaches.

The visual component of Facebook Ads is crucial. Design eye-catching visuals that clearly convey your book's genre and appeal. A professional book cover paired with a short, compelling message can stop scrolling thumbs in their tracks. For instance, for a revamped classic, you might craft an ad with the tagline, "Rediscover the mystery you love—with modern twists!" Alongside the imagery, test different calls to action, such as "Order Now," "Learn More," or "Download a Free Sample," to see what resonates most with your audience.

To truly harness the power of paid ads, consistency is vital. Start with small budgets and run A/B tests to compare different creatives, targeting options, and copy. Track the results and use the data to refine your campaigns incrementally. Pay attention to key metrics like engagement, click-through rates, and conversion rates. If one audience or ad set underperforms, adjust and pivot rather than abandoning the tactic entirely.

Remember, effective advertising isn't just about spending money to get seen; it's about understanding who your audience is, meeting them where they are, and inviting them into the unique reading experience your book offers. With focus and persistence, paid ads can transform your public domain project from a passion into a profitable success.

Reaching Niche Audiences Effectively

Niche audiences have the potential to become a powerful catalyst for your book's success. Unlike mainstream markets, where competition can be overwhelming, niche categories provide opportunities to connect with highly engaged, passionate readers who are eager for specific content. By focusing on well-defined themes, genres, or special interests, you can position your book as the perfect fit for a smaller but intensely loyal audience.

The first step in reaching niche audiences is to identify the most relevant aspect of your book that aligns with their interests. Consider your public domain work's themes, historical context, or reimagined features. For example, if your book is a uniquely illustrated edition of a classic fairy tale, it could appeal to art enthusiasts, children's literature fans, or collectors of beautifully designed books. If you've adapted a public domain text into a modern-day self-help guide, your audience might include professionals, students, or individuals exploring personal growth.

Social media platforms are an excellent way to directly interact with these communities. Platforms like Instagram, Facebook, and TikTok host vibrant niche communities that center around specific topics. Instagram hashtags can help you discover micro-communities, such as #HistoricalFictionFans or #BookIllustrationLovers. Engage with these communities by sharing posts that showcase your book's highlights, such as its unique packaging, visually enticing elements, or a behind-the-scenes look at how you brought it to life. TikTok, particularly through BookTok, is another incredible tool for niche engagement. Posting short, creative videos about your book's features or its historical or cultural significance can capture the attention of enthusiastic readers scrolling through their feeds.

Forums and subreddits remain invaluable for finding niche audiences with shared interests. Subreddits like r/BookCollecting, r/Literature, or specific genre-focused subreddits like r/SciFiBooks are perfect avenues to begin authentic conversations about your work. Join discussions, contribute insights, and share your passion for the subject before introducing your book as something that appeals to the group's shared interests. Avoid blatant self-promotion. Instead, focus on gaining trust and adding value, which will naturally create interest in your book.

Book clubs and reading communities can also become important allies in your niche-marketing efforts. Reach out to these groups and demonstrate how your book aligns with their preferences. For example, a public domain book expertly adapted into a teacher's guide is a natural fit for educational book clubs, either in-person or online.

Contact schools, libraries, and homeschooling associations to present your book as a resource educators and parents can benefit from. Craft a personalized pitch highlighting how your book simplifies teaching or enhances learning experiences for their students.

Local or specialized events and meetups are another pathway to connect with niche readers in person. If your book resonates with history enthusiasts, setting up a booth at a local historical society's fair or museum event could generate both excitement and sales. Alternatively, unique books like those exploring niche hobbies or lifestyle themes can find success at craft fairs or conventions dedicated to those subjects.

Finally, don't underestimate the power of niche influencers. Look for bloggers, YouTubers, or Instagram personalities who cater to specific audiences that align with your book. For instance, a creator who reviews illustrated books or explores rare literary collections might partner with you to feature your release. By leveraging their already engaged audience, your book gains increased credibility and exposure.

At the heart of niche marketing is authentic connection. Building trust and relationships with these communities is just as important as promoting your book. The more you genuinely engage with these groups, offering content and conversation that resonates, the more they'll be inclined to support your work and recommend it to others. When done right, niche audiences don't simply become buyers; they transform into advocates, spreading the word about your book in ways no traditional campaign could achieve.

Leveraging the Power of Influencer Marketing

Influencer marketing isn't just a tool for major corporations; it's a priceless strategy for authors aiming to expand their readership without breaking the bank. By tapping into the power of influencers who already speak directly to your ideal audience, you can amplify your book's visibility and credibility. The key is fostering genuine collaborations that benefit both the influencer and the readers they serve.

Start by identifying influencers, bloggers, podcasters, or YouTubers who align naturally with your book's content and target audience. For example, if you've adapted a public domain text into a new illustrated edition, seek out influencers who specialize in reviewing children's literature, book art, or collectible editions. Similarly, if your work resonates with a specific niche, like self-help or historical fiction, find influencers immersed in those topics. Tools like Instagram, Twitter, and even niche platforms like Goodreads can help you discover content creators whose audience aligns with your book's themes.

When reaching out to influencers, focus on building a relationship rather than immediately pitching your book. Begin by engaging with their content—like, comment, and share posts that resonate with you. This will help you understand their style and audience before making contact. When you're ready to communicate, craft a personalized message that highlights why their platform is a great fit for your book. Be specific about what you admire and how your collaboration can bring value to their followers. For instance, you might write, "I love how you highlight unique perspectives in your book reviews, and I think my annotated classic edition of X would resonate with your audience who appreciates updated takes on timeless literature."

One of the most accessible approaches is to offer influencers free review copies of your book. Along with the book, include a thoughtful letter expressing why you believe their audience will enjoy it. For example, "I've reimagined this classic with modern illustrations and side-by-side commentary to make it more engaging for today's readers. I thought your artistic and literary audience might find it compelling."

Allow influencers to give honest reviews and share them on their platforms, as authentic opinions are far more impactful than scripted endorsements.

Organizing giveaways in collaboration with influencers is another creative way to gain visibility. Offer free copies of your book to their followers as part of a contest or promotion. For example, an influencer might post, "I'm thrilled to partner with [Your Name] to give away three copies of this beautifully illustrated edition of X! To enter, follow both of us and comment below your favorite classic read." This approach not only increases engagement but also introduces your book to a wider audience in a fun, memorable way.

Micro-influencers, who typically have smaller, highly engaged followings, can often make a bigger impact than larger influencers with wider audiences. Their followers trust their recommendations and interact more actively with their posts, which can translate into higher conversion rates. A niche book blogger with 5,000 dedicated readers, for instance, might result in more sales than a general influencer with 100,000 followers. Leverage this by seeking out micro-influencers who are passionate about your book's genre or themes and who regularly interact with their audience.

To maximize collaboration, think beyond book reviews. Suggest participating in a live Q&A session on Instagram or YouTube, where you can discuss your book's unique elements and answer audience questions. Or provide the influencer with exclusive content, such as excerpts, behind-the-scenes details, or bonus materials they can share with their followers. For example, "Did you know this updated edition includes never-before-seen illustrations that bring the story to life?"

Lastly, track and measure the results of your influencer collaborations. Note increases in book sales, social media engagement, or website traffic after a campaign. Use this data to refine future influencer partnerships and focus on the platforms and strategies that yield the best results.

Influencer marketing works so well because it's based on trust and relatability. Followers look to these creators as tastemakers, valuing their opinions as though they're from a trusted friend. When you collaborate with influencers thoughtfully and authentically, you're not just spreading the word about your book. You're creating meaningful connections with readers, sparking interest, and fostering lasting engagement with your work.

Optimizing Your Product Descriptions for Maximum Impact

Your product description isn't just a rundown of your book's content; it's a persuasive tool designed to capture interest, spark desire, and ultimately drive purchases. This small section of text plays an outsized role in turning potential customers into readers. A great description doesn't just tell people what your book is about; it vividly shows them why they need it.

The first few lines of your description are critical, as they serve as the hook. Most online platforms show only the opening lines before a user has to click "Read More," so these sentences must grab attention. Start with something bold and enticing. For example, pose a compelling question that intrigues the reader, such as, "What if the key to your happiness was hidden in a story written over a century ago?" Alternatively, use an intriguing statement or promise, such as, "Rediscover a timeless classic like you've never seen it before—with illustrations and insights that breathe fresh life into every page."

Once you've hooked the reader, your description should flow seamlessly into addressing their needs, desires, or pain points. Think like your audience. Why are they searching for a book like yours? Are they looking to be entertained, seeking to expand their knowledge, or hoping to relive the magic of a literary classic? Tailor your description to meet those emotional or practical needs. For example, if you're selling a modern adaptation of a public domain mystery novel, draw the reader in by saying, "Step into a world of intrigue and danger as this meticulously reimagined classic takes you on a heart-pounding adventure."

To maintain engagement, clearly articulate how your book stands out and delivers value. Highlight the unique features or enhancements you've added to your adaptation. Is it an annotated version designed to make complex ideas accessible to modern readers? Does it include illustrations that transport readers into another era? Perhaps you've restructured the text to improve its flow for contemporary audiences. Don't just tell readers what your book is; show them how it enriches their experience. For instance, you might emphasize, "This edition includes commentary that unpacks the symbolism and cultural context, allowing readers to appreciate this masterpiece like never before."

Effective product descriptions also leverage powerful emotional language. Use words and phrases that evoke curiosity, excitement, or connection. Replace flat statements like "This book is a great read" with something vivid and emotional, such as, "Prepare to be swept away into a story that's as hauntingly beautiful now as it was a century ago."

To maximize the reach of your product description, keywords are non-negotiable. Research phrases your target audience might search for, such as "classic literature with modern commentary," "best illustrated editions," or "vintage mysteries for new readers." Incorporate these terms naturally into your description without making it read like a keyword dump. Strategically placing these words in the opening lines, middle, and closing of your text ensures search algorithms catch them, boosting your book's visibility on platforms like Amazon.

Structuring your description for readability is another essential element. Break up your text into digestible sections using short paragraphs and, where applicable, bolded phrases or capitalized highlights. This makes it easier for readers to skim yet still grasp the most important details.

Finally, consider ending your description with a clear and irresistible call to action. This could be something direct such as, "Order your copy today and rediscover a classic in a whole new way." Or it can be tailored to the emotional connection you've established, like, "Don't miss your chance to own the edition that will make you fall in love with this timeless story all over again."

A well-crafted product description can transform interest into action. By understanding your audience, hooking them early, reinforcing the unique value your book offers, and optimizing for visibility, you're giving your book the best possible chance to stand out in a crowded marketplace.

Driving Engagement Through Social Media

Social media is one of the most powerful tools at your disposal for generating excitement around your repurposed public domain book. Platforms like Instagram, Twitter, and TikTok aren't just places for casual socializing; they're vibrant hubs where readers discover, connect with, and share their favorite books. Leveraging these platforms strategically can make all the difference in sparking curiosity, driving engagement, and building a community of loyal readers.

The key to success on social media is consistency, creativity, and understanding the unique dynamics of each platform. Tailor your approach to match the strengths and expectations of the audience on Instagram, Twitter, TikTok, or whichever platform you choose to focus on.

Instagram

Instagram offers a visual-first approach that's perfect for showcasing the visual appeal of your book. If your repurposed public domain book has unique features, such as stunning illustrations, artistic cover designs, or intriguing annotations, this is the place to shine. Post high-quality images of the book cover, close-ups of illustrations, or aesthetic flat lays featuring your book alongside thematic props.

Use Instagram Stories and Reels to create bite-sized content that keeps followers engaged. For example, you can film a short video flipping through the pages and highlighting a favorite excerpt or comment on what inspired your adaptation. Behind-the-scenes content always resonates well here. Document the process of modernizing your book through short clips or time-lapse videos of brainstorming sessions, design work, or editing rounds.

Hashtags like #Bookstagram, #ClassicBooks, and niche-specific tags like #MysteryNovels or #HistoricalFiction are your allies. Add these to your posts to help readers passionate about your genre discover your content. Encourage followers to tag you in posts when they receive or read your book, creating a sense of community and further exposure.

Twitter

Twitter thrives on quick communication and meaningful conversations. This makes it an ideal platform for sparking discussions about your book's themes, historical significance, or relevance to modern audiences. Share interesting facts or anecdotes about the public domain work you've adapted. For instance, tweet something like, "Did you know this mysterious character in [Book] inspired a famous detective in modern fiction? Discover more in my updated edition!"

Participating in weekly hashtags like #WriterWednesday, #BookLovers, or #CreativeCorner can help amplify your reach. Additionally, live-tweeting relevant events, such as book-related anniversaries or trending conversations in your genre, positions you as an engaged and knowledgeable creator within your niche.

Don't hesitate to interact directly with your audience. Respond to comments, participate in polls, or initiate threads that invite others to share their favorite moments from the original version of your book. A question like, "What's your favorite quote from [classic book]? Mine is ___," can open up meaningful dialogue and engagement.

TikTok

TikTok, particularly through BookTok, has revolutionized how books gain visibility, especially among younger audiences. The platform thrives on authentic, relatable, and often humorous content. Create videos that highlight what makes your book unique. For example, present a "before and after" transformation that showcases the original public domain text alongside your updated, modernized version. Or, try a quirky trend, such as "5 Reasons Why You Should Try [Book Title]."

Storytelling videos work especially well. You could narrate a quick recap of the book's history or a fascinating tidbit about its themes while adding entertaining visuals, text overlays, and music. Be sure to introduce your book with energy and creativity, such as holding it up with, "What if I told you THIS classic holds the secret to ___?"

Capture the TikTok audience's penchant for challenges and interaction. Propose something like a #TimelessClassicChallenge, where followers take a scene from your book and imagine it playing out in the modern day. A hashtag featuring your book name, like #RediscoverBookTitle, helps establish a unique connection to your content.

Engaging Content Ideas

Regardless of platform, variety is key. Here are specific ideas to keep your content fresh and engaging:

- **Behind-the-Scenes Insights:** Share the "why" behind your decision to transform this particular classic. Explain your creative process, such as updating language or adding new illustrations.

- **Excerpt Highlights:** Post short passages from your book with a visually striking background or accompanying voiceover. Focus on parts that provoke curiosity or hook readers emotionally.

- **Reader Spotlights:** Reshare posts from readers who mention or feature your book. Show your appreciation, and use their excitement to build credibility for your work.

- **Collaborations:** Partner with other authors, illustrators, or creators in your genre to co-host events like live Q&As, virtual book clubs, or reading challenges.

Building Relationships Through Social Media

Social media thrives on interaction. It's not just a broadcast platform; it's a space where real relationships are developed. Host live Q&A sessions to answer questions from followers, giving them direct access to your insights. For example, "Join me this Friday for a live chat about my new illustrated edition of [Book]! Got burning questions about the original story or my process? Drop them below!"

Engage in hashtags and communities your audience frequents, such as #ClassicLit or #BookAdaptations. Comment thoughtfully on other users' posts to build rapport rather than promotion. And when someone praises your book publicly, take the time to thank them or start a conversation. Authenticity in your interactions builds trust and loyalty over time.

Social media isn't merely about shouting into the void; it's about starting conversations, telling compelling stories, and showing the world why your book matters. By focusing on the strengths of specific platforms and creating authentic, engaging content, you'll cultivate an audience eager to engage with your work, support your vision, and share your book with others. Patience and persistence are key—but when done thoughtfully, social media becomes a powerful driver of your book's success.

Turning Customers into Advocates

Your readers are not just consumers; they can become your most powerful advocates if you nurture the connection. A satisfied reader who takes the time to recommend your book can drive interest, boost credibility, and even spark a chain reaction of word-of-mouth marketing.

By turning customers into passionate advocates, you're creating an army of promoters who feel personally invested in your book's success.

Encourage Positive Reviews with Thoughtful Requests

Positive reviews are critical for building credibility and attracting new readers. However, many satisfied readers need a little nudge to leave reviews, so make it easy for them. At the end of your book, include a concise but polite call-to-action, such as, "If you enjoyed this book, I'd love to hear your thoughts! Leaving a quick review helps others discover it too." Pair this with a link directing them to the review page on Amazon, Goodreads, or another relevant platform. The easier you make it, the more likely readers are to follow through.

You can also use follow-up emails to thank readers for their purchase and invite them to share their experience. Frame this as a conversation rather than a demand. For example, "I hope you enjoyed [Book Title]! If you have a moment, I'd love to hear what you thought. Your feedback not only helps me grow but also helps other readers find their next favorite book."

For maximum impact, show appreciation when someone leaves a review. A simple thank-you message or comment in response to their feedback can go a long way in reinforcing their role as a valued part of your book's community.

Build a Community Around Your Book

Creating a sense of community transforms casual readers into loyal supporters who feel connected to your work. This starts with offering opportunities for ongoing engagement. Consider launching an email newsletter that delivers regular updates, behind-the-scenes glimpses, or exclusive content. For example, send out "hidden chapters," discussion guides, or fun trivia about the book and its creation to keep readers feeling included.

Social media can also play a vital role in fostering community. Create a Facebook group, subreddit, or hashtag specific to your book where readers can share their thoughts, discuss themes, and connect with each other. Encourage interaction with prompts like, "Who was your favorite character in [Book Title], and why?" or "What alternate ending would you have written for this story?" Actively participating in these discussions yourself adds a personal touch and makes readers feel closer to you as an author.

You might also consider hosting virtual events, such as live Q&A sessions, readings, or book club discussions, where readers can interact directly with you and each other. These interactions deepen the relationship and strengthen their enthusiasm for your book.

Incentivize Advocacy Through Exclusive Rewards

Offering special perks or recognition to your most engaged supporters can turn them into vocal advocates for your book. Set up a referral program where readers who recommend your book to friends receive a free digital asset, such as a bookmark, downloadable artwork, or bonus chapter. For example, "Send this book to three friends, and you'll receive an exclusive short story featuring [a beloved character]."

Exclusive content like advanced previews of future books or author insights as part of a "loyal reader club" can also make readers feel valued. Give them sneak peeks, share personal notes about the creative process, or even credit their contributions publicly, such as in an acknowledgments section of your next edition.

If your book is part of a larger adaptation or series, foster excitement around the brand by sharing updates on social media that keep readers in the loop. Offering special promotions, signed copies, or limited-edition merchandise tied to your book rewards loyalty and builds anticipation.

Cultivate Word-of-Mouth Marketing

One of the simplest ways to turn readers into advocates is to make it easy for them to talk about your book. Include shareable assets in your emails or online materials, such as pre-written social media posts, eye-catching visuals, or hashtags. For example, create an Instagram-friendly graphic with a popular quote from the book and encourage readers to share it with their followers.

You might even encourage fans to post about their reading experience by running contests or challenges, such as a photo challenge where they share a creative picture of your book in their space or a video review on TikTok. Recognize and celebrate those who participate by resharing their posts or entering them into giveaways.

Reviews, recommendations, and shared posts become even more valuable when you make an effort to highlight and thank your advocates publicly. A simple comment like, "Thank you for sharing! I'm thrilled to hear you enjoyed [Book Title]" creates goodwill and reinforces their enthusiasm for your work.

Create a Lasting Impression

At the core of turning customers into advocates is the relationship you build with them. Readers become passionate supporters when they feel they've received exceptional value and can connect emotionally with your story. Focus on delivering consistent quality, engaging genuinely with your audience, and showing appreciation at every step.

With time and care, these strategies do more than boost sales. They cultivate lasting relationships and transform your book marketing into a vibrant, self-sustaining engine fueled by enthusiastic readers. Ultimately, advocacy creates a ripple effect, helping your public domain adaptation reach heart after heart, bookshelf after bookshelf.

Chapter Nine

Scaling Up and Diversifying Income Streams

When your first steps in public domain publishing prove successful, a world of new possibilities opens up. You've laid the groundwork by identifying and revitalizing a hidden gem, but success doesn't have to stop at a single book. The next logical question is, how can you take this momentum and turn it into something greater? The answer lies in scaling up and diversifying your efforts. Scaling allows you to produce more with less effort, optimizing your processes so you can focus on growth and creativity. Diversification, on the other hand, helps safeguard your business by creating multiple streams of income, ensuring stability and resilience even when the market shifts.

Imagine this: your first project resonated with a niche audience. Perhaps it was a beautifully designed adaptation of a forgotten mystery novel or a modernized version of a timeless textbook. But now, instead of treating it as a one-time win, you can build upon it. Maybe you expand it into a broader series, offer additional formats such as audiobooks or collector's editions, or even create exclusive content to deepen engagement. These steps not only maximize the value of your initial work but also set the stage for long-term success.

Scaling up isn't just about doing more; it's about doing things smarter. By automating repetitive tasks or outsourcing specialized work, you free yourself to focus on bigger-picture strategies, such as curating collections or creating complementary offerings. Meanwhile, diversification can bring entirely new dimensions to your business. A single book can evolve into a full-fledged brand with educational tie-ins, subscription-based content, or even workshops that teach others how to unlock the public domain's potential.

The goal of scaling and diversifying isn't to overextend yourself but to ensure that your efforts are sustainable, adaptable, and impactful. This chapter will walk you through actionable strategies to streamline your operations, expand your reach, and explore new income opportunities, all without sacrificing the creativity and passion that brought you into this venture in the first place. By the time you've finished, you'll have a clear roadmap for transforming a single book into a thriving business capable of reaching new heights.

Automating Processes for Greater Efficiency

When it comes to building a scalable and sustainable business, efficiency is your best friend. The more streamlined your operations, the more time and mental space you'll have to focus on the creative and strategic aspects of your publishing venture. Automation is the key to freeing yourself from repetitive, time-consuming tasks so you can prioritize the elements that truly move the needle. Tools, systems, and smart delegation can make all the difference in taking your publishing business to new heights.

Streamlining Book Production

The process of producing books, whether they're eBooks, paperbacks, or audiobooks, can quickly become overwhelming without the right tools. Thankfully, platforms like Vellum and Atticus simplify this process dramatically. These tools allow you to turn your manuscript into professionally formatted eBooks and print-ready files in a matter of minutes. You don't need to be a design expert or spend hours tweaking layouts. The software generates clean, attractive formats that are compatible with major retailers like Amazon Kindle, Apple Books, and more, ensuring your books meet all technical requirements.

Similarly, audiobook production doesn't have to be a time sink when you outsource to skilled freelancers. Websites like ACX make it easy to connect with professional narrators who can bring your adaptations to life, leaving you free to focus on your next project. Outsourcing these steps doesn't just save time; it enhances the quality of your final product, making it more appealing to readers and listeners alike.

Automating Reader Engagement

Connecting with your audience is one of the most critical aspects of growing your business—but it can also be one of the most time-consuming. Thankfully, email marketing platforms like Mailchimp, ConvertKit, or ActiveCampaign allow you to automate this process while keeping it personal. A well-designed welcome sequence can start building a relationship with new subscribers the moment they join your email list. This sequence might include a warm introduction, updates about your current and upcoming projects, and a free bonus, such as an exclusive short story or a printable reading guide. By automating these emails, you stay top of mind without needing to micromanage.

Once your welcome sequence is set up, you can expand on automation by creating segmented email campaigns tailored to specific reader interests. For example, one group might receive updates on an upcoming collection of mystery novellas, while another gets sneak peeks at an audiobook adaptation. These automated workflows ensure your communication remains relevant, timely, and impactful.

Simplifying Social Media

Social media presence is vital for visibility in the crowded publishing space, but managing accounts across multiple platforms can become a full-time job. Tools like Buffer, Hootsuite, and Later allow you to schedule posts well in advance, ensuring a steady stream of content without requiring daily attention. Imagine dedicating a single day each month to crafting posts, uploading them to a scheduling tool, and letting the platform handle the rest. This approach ensures consistency in your marketing efforts, even as you juggle other tasks.

Smart scheduling also allows you to experiment with content types and posting times to see what resonates best with your audience. For example, you might promote an upcoming release by sharing excerpts, behind-the-scenes anecdotes, or artwork. Over time, analytics from these tools can help you refine your social media strategy, concentrating your efforts where they have the most impact.

Delegating Specialized Tasks

No entrepreneur can wear every hat, and trying to do so often leads to burnout or subpar results. Delegating specialized tasks to experienced freelancers is a smart way to maintain high standards while focusing your energy on things only you can do. For instance, a skilled graphic designer can create stunning covers or promotional materials that stand out in the marketplace, while a freelance editor ensures your final manuscript is polished and professional. Platforms like Fiverr, Upwork, and 99designs provide access to talented professionals who can deliver high-quality results within your budget.

Alongside outsourcing creative tasks, consider hiring a virtual assistant (VA) to handle administrative responsibilities. A VA can help with email management, research, customer service, and other time-consuming tasks, which lets you focus on crafting new adaptations or curating collections.

The Long-Term Benefits of Automation

The true power of automation lies in its ability to create a system that works even when you're not actively managing every detail. By automating processes, you free yourself from operational bottlenecks and position your business for sustainable growth. Whether it's through email sequences that work around the clock, tools that streamline your book production, or freelancers who enhance the quality of your work, automation lets you scale effectively without sacrificing creativity or sanity.

Efficiency is not about cutting corners; it's about optimizing the way you spend your time and energy. With the right tools and strategies, you can accomplish more in less time, ensuring consistency, quality, and the mental bandwidth to innovate. Automation is not just a tool for large corporations; it's a necessity for publishers looking to scale their efforts and maximize their impact in the world of public domain adaptations.

Expanding from Single Titles to Series and Brands

One of the most effective ways to scale your public domain publishing efforts is by transforming the success of individual projects into wider-reaching series or cohesive brands. This strategy not only builds on existing momentum but also deepens your engagement with audiences who crave continuity and consistency. If a single book resonates with your readers, why stop there? By strategically designing related releases, you can create an enriched experience for your audience and significantly boost your income potential.

Creating Series from Successful Titles

Public domain works often lend themselves naturally to becoming part of a series, particularly when they involve recurring characters, linked narratives, or thematic connections. Consider the timeless popularity of Sherlock Holmes stories. Each tale can be released individually, but when bundled into a complete series with a unified design and consistent branding, the appeal for fans and collectors grows exponentially. The same can be said for literary classics like Jane Austen's novels, which can be reimagined as a matching set with cohesive cover art and complementary designs.

To amplify the appeal of your series, you can add value by including bonus content that enhances the reading experience. For example, appendices with historical context, maps, family trees for characters, or author notes act as compelling selling points. Additionally, serialized content can create anticipation among readers who will eagerly await the next installment. If you're adapting period-poetry collections, for example, releasing them in incremental volumes allows you to maintain a steady publication pace and keep your audience engaged over time.

Leveraging Thematic Collections and Anthologies

Thematic collections are another way to expand your catalog while offering readers a curated experience. By grouping public domain works around a central theme, audience interest can be heightened when they see the added value of a well-thought-out collection. For instance, you might compile classic mystery tales into a detective anthology, perfect for fans of intrigue and suspense. Other examples include bundling Gothic horror stories for Halloween enthusiasts or assembling inspirational poetry aimed at readers searching for motivation.

These collections allow you to tap into specific niche audiences. Consider creating anthologies for special occasions, like a romantic compilation for Valentine's Day or a cozy winter-themed set for the holiday season. Pairing thoughtful curation with beautiful packaging, such as unique fonts or illustrated book covers, ensures your offerings are set apart in a saturated marketplace. Thematic compilations make wonderful gifts as well, widening their appeal for holiday shoppers or special event purchases.

Developing Your Public Domain Brand

Beyond individual titles and collections, establishing a recognizable brand can elevate your work to new heights and allow you to build lasting relationships with your readers. Branding gives all your projects a cohesive and professional feel, while also setting expectations for your audience. For example, if your brand centers around crafting luxury collector's editions of beloved literary classics, readers will come to associate your name with top-tier design, quality binding, and one-of-a-kind embellishments.

To begin crafting your brand, first identify your niche. Do you specialize in illustrated children's books based on fairy tales? Are you creating modernized, annotated versions of classic literature for academic use? Or perhaps your focus is on premium hardcover collections aimed at book collectors? Once you've defined your niche, ensure your branding elements, such as logo designs, typography, and website aesthetic, reflect a consistent look and feel.

Branding goes beyond visuals. Consider your brand's voice and mission. For instance, your mission might be to make timeless stories accessible to modern readers who appreciate beautifully packaged editions. Communicating this through social media, newsletters, or even the "About" page of your website builds trust and makes your audience feel part of a larger narrative.

Offering Added Value Through Extras

To solidify your brand and make your works even more appealing, think about extras that enrich the reader's experience. For example, adding audio or video components can make a book version stand out. Audio introductions or commentaries contextualizing a text provide motivation for buyers seeking a more interactive experience. If you brand yourself as catering to academics, including study guides, historical analysis, or worksheets can further position you as an educational resource.

Another idea is to create limited-edition products that become collector's items. These might include hand-bound or leather-bound volumes with unique designs, foil embossing, and ribbon bookmarks. For fans of public domain classics, these added touches are worth premium pricing and elevate your brand as a leader in quality and attention to detail.

Maintaining Momentum with Consistent Engagement

Expansion doesn't mean neglecting the audience that initially supported you; consistency is crucial to building loyalty. Maintain regular communication through email newsletters, surveys (to understand what readers want next), and blogs sharing behind-the-scenes details about your creative process. Celebrate milestones in your series' growth, like the release of a new volume or reaching a sales goal, to keep your audience invested and excited about what's next.

The Power of Scaling Through Series and Brands

By turning single titles into interconnected series, thematic collections, or fully-fledged brands, you create a steady foundation for long-term success. Readers crave immersion, and nothing satisfies like a well-planned series of books or a consistently delightful brand experience. Combine this approach with thoughtful design, clear mission statements, and added value to elevate your public domain publishing efforts from individual projects to an empire readers will remember. Whatever direction you choose, these efforts are about more than just scaling up; they're about crafting a legacy within the public domain space.

Diversifying Revenue Streams

Relying on a single source of income can put even the most well-run business at risk when market conditions change. Diversification is not merely a safeguard; it also unlocks untapped opportunities that can significantly boost your earnings and strengthen your business model. By exploring various revenue streams connected to your public domain offerings, you not only generate stability but also broaden your audience reach and engagement. Whether through subscription models, licensing agreements, or hands-on workshops, there are endless ways to bring in consistent income while adding value for your audience.

Building Subscription Models for Recurring Revenue

One of the most impactful ways to diversify your income is through subscription-based models. These programs create a steady and predictable revenue stream, while also cultivating deeper loyalty from your audience. For instance, you might develop a literary membership club where subscribers gain access to exclusive content not available elsewhere. Imagine patrons receiving beautifully annotated eBooks, serialized releases of rare stories, or even early access to upcoming projects. These perks not only reward existing fans but also make your subscription offering a coveted, premium experience.

To enhance the appeal, include interactive components. For example, host monthly virtual book club meetings or live Q&A sessions where subscribers can get to know you and discuss the works you've published. You could even offer tiered memberships, with higher levels granting access to collectibles, signed editions, or one-of-a-kind extras like custom illustrations inspired by the books. Platforms like Patreon,

Substack, or your own e-commerce site make it easier than ever to get started and customize your offerings.

Exploring Opportunities in Licensing Agreements

Licensing is a powerful way to extend the reach of your adaptations while creating new revenue streams. Libraries, museums, and schools are often eager to acquire rights to distribute or showcase high-quality adaptations of public domain works. For example, licensing your works as educational materials allows schools to incorporate them into curriculums, especially if they've been enhanced with annotations, historical context, or study guides. Similarly, libraries may be interested in digital editions or printed volumes for their patrons, particularly if they fill a niche not widely represented in their collections.

You could also approach museums or cultural organizations. Imagine working with an art museum to create a curated edition of relevant poetry or prose to accompany a special exhibit. Licensing could extend to digital platforms as well, such as licensing your works to audiobook publishers or streaming platforms. This approach not only expands exposure to new audiences but also establishes long-term partnerships that bolster your business's credibility within academic, cultural, or entertainment sectors.

Sharing Expertise Through Workshops and Courses

Another compelling route to diversify income is to share what you know with others eager to enter the world of public domain publishing. Workshops and courses are highly engaging ways to monetize your knowledge while establishing yourself as a thought leader in this unique niche. Aspiring creators, educators, and entrepreneurs can benefit from your insights, especially when it comes to selecting works to adapt, understanding copyright guidelines, or mastering the publishing process.

Online workshops offer scalability and convenience. Platforms like Teachable, Skillshare, or Zoom make it easy to design and deliver courses on topics like "How to Curate Public Domain Works" or "Building a Brand Through Classic Literature." You might also create pre-recorded series that participants can purchase and watch at their own pace, allowing you to generate passive income.

For those who prefer face-to-face interaction, local universities, community centers, or writing groups present opportunities for in-person workshops. Imagine hosting a weekend seminar where attendees walk away with actionable plans for launching their own public domain projects or even work alongside you to create their first adaptation. These events not only bring in additional revenue but create a network of peers and collaborators who expand your reach even further.

Adding Value Through Premium Experiences

To take full advantage of your diversified streams, consider bundling these offerings into premium experiences. For instance, a high-level membership package might include access to exclusive workshops combined with digital bonus content and collectible editions of your works. Or, a licensing partnership with educational institutions could include a subscription-like model where they receive new editions or series updates annually.

Premium branding helps reinforce the value of these diversified avenues. If you're offering workshops, ensure they are professionally designed and consistently branded in line with your other projects.

Collaborate with industry experts or instructors for additional credibility and polish. By focusing on high-quality delivery across all channels, each revenue stream enhances the other, building momentum for your brand as a whole.

Why Diversification Matters

The beauty of diversification lies in its ability to protect and expand your business simultaneously. By combining subscription models, licensing opportunities, and paid workshops, you reduce reliance on any one income stream and create a more adaptable and resilient business capable of weathering market changes. These efforts don't just lead to financial rewards; they deepen your connection with your audience, allowing more people to experience the timeless works you've brought back to life. Ultimately, diversification positions your brand as both an income generator and an innovator within the rich world of public domain publishing.##

Collaborating to Broaden Appeal

Collaboration has the potential to breathe new life into your public domain publishing projects, elevating them from simple adaptations to multidimensional works of art. When you partner with creatives in complementary areas, the possibilities for innovation and enhanced audience reach are endless. Whether you work with illustrators, writers, educators, or other professionals, collaboration can result in projects that are fresh, engaging, and highly marketable.

Partnering with Illustrators to Create Visual Appeal

Illustrations can transform a text-based project into a visual master-piece. Collaborating with an artist allows you to create beautifully illustrated editions that appeal to a broader audience. For example, a public domain fairy tale adorned with whimsical, hand-drawn artwork can captivate children and parents alike. Similarly, intricate illustrations for classics like Lewis Carroll's *Alice's Adventures in Wonderland* or Edgar Allan Poe's *The Raven* might entice collectors and book enthusiasts seeking unique, high-quality editions.

Illustrators also bring their distinct styles to the table, helping your editions stand out in a visually crowded marketplace. Whether you choose a modern, minimalist approach or ornate, period-inspired designs, the right artwork can align your project with current trends or niche interests. Collaborating on limited-edition releases, complete with custom covers, gold embossing, or even signed prints, can attract gift buyers or collectors willing to pay premium prices.

Adding Depth with Writers and Experts

Some readers gravitate toward works that offer more than just the text itself. By teaming up with writers or subject matter experts, you can add layers of value to your adaptations. Consider including forewords, essays, or contemporary commentary that situates a work in its historical or cultural context. These additions can appeal to readers who enjoy deeper insights, making your editions a natural choice for academic readers or enthusiasts of classic literature.

For instance, pairing a public domain novel with a modern feminist analysis or historical timeline can open up broader conversations and draw in more diverse audiences. Writers or critics could also collaborate on annotated editions, enriching the text with notes that explain obscure references, language, or settings. This gives your work a unique edge and positions it as both an educational resource and an entertaining read.

Collaborating with Educators for Academic Impact

Educators can help you adapt your projects for use in schools and universities, creating tailored materials that align with curriculums. For example, a teacher might work with you to develop lesson plans, discussion questions, or quizzes to accompany a novel like *Pride and Prejudice*. Including these resources as part of your offerings makes your books an obvious choice for educators seeking ready-made solutions for their classrooms.

Collaboration with educators also opens the door to licensing opportunities. Schools are often willing to pay for specialized editions that support their curriculum objectives, whether in digital or print format. With the right partnerships, your work can become a go-to resource for academic institutions, ensuring a steady stream of revenue and elevating your status in the educational sector.

Expanding Reach Through Collaborative Networks

The most immediate benefit of collaborating with others is the opportunity to tap into their networks. A well-established illustrator will likely have fans who eagerly follow their work, and these fans may become your readers, too. Similarly, educators, writers, and critics often have professional or academic communities that trust their recommendations. By working together, you multiply your visibility and credibility in ways that could take years to achieve alone.

Collaboration isn't limited to creation; promotional partnerships can also extend your reach. Co-hosting events like virtual book launches, live drawing sessions, or guest lecture series can amplify awareness of your projects. Each partner's audience becomes a shared pool of potential readers and supporters, significantly broadening your appeal.

The Long-Term Benefits of Collaboration

Collaboration is an investment in quality, creativity, and growth that pays dividends over time. By working with other experts, you expose your projects to fresh perspectives and innovative ideas that might otherwise go untapped. The partnerships you build also have the potential to evolve into long-term professional relationships, further enriching your work and expanding your opportunities. Most importantly, collaboration positions your projects as high-value offerings that resonate with diverse audiences.

Building a Sustainable and Scalable Future

Scaling up your public domain publishing efforts isn't just about doing more; it's about doing it smarter. Creating a sustainable, long-term business means carefully balancing innovation and efficiency at every stage, ensuring your work keeps growing without compromising on quality or vision. By focusing on scalable practices and diversified revenue streams, you can establish a foundation that supports ongoing success.

Prioritizing Sustainable Workflows

At the heart of sustainability lies efficiency. Streamlined workflows make it easier to manage multiple projects and ensure consistent output without feeling overwhelmed. For instance, automating tasks like eBook formatting or creating templates for social media promotion saves time and energy that you can reinvest in strategy or creativity.

Batching tasks is another sustainable approach. Instead of switching between activities, dedicate specific days or weeks to certain tasks, such as designing covers, planning marketing campaigns, or curating new manuscripts. This reduces mental fatigue, boosts productivity, and creates a rhythm that keeps your operations running smoothly.

Scaling Thoughtfully Through Series and Collections

One of the cornerstones of scalability is thoughtful expansion through series and collections. By designing cohesive sets of books, you create opportunities for repeat purchases and sustained reader interest. Whether it's releasing part two of a serialized story or curating a multi-volume anthology around a theme, each new installment builds on the momentum of the last.

Additionally, collection-building invites exploration of audience niches. A series of public domain mysteries might resonate with one group, while a collection of illustrated fairy tales appeals to another. By identifying and catering to these niches, you sustainably expand your audience without overextending your resources.

Diversifying Revenue for Greater Resilience

Sustainability is closely tied to financial security, which is where diversified income streams come into play. By combining book sales with subscriptions, licensing agreements, merchandise, and educational offerings, you create a robust ecosystem that isn't overly dependent on one product or market. This resilience ensures your business can adapt to changes while staying profitable.

For example, while book sales might experience seasonal fluctuations, monthly subscription revenue or workshop fees can provide a consistent baseline of income. Similarly, licensing your adaptations to academic institutions or digital platforms opens channels for passive earnings that complement your direct-to-reader sales.

Remaining True to Your Vision

Even as you scale and diversify, it's important to remain anchored to the mission and vision that inspire your work. Whether it's making timeless literature accessible, curating rare texts, or creating visually stunning editions, your unique perspective is what draws and retains your audience. Every strategic decision—from choosing automation tools to forming new partnerships—should align with this core vision.

Leaving a Legacy

Growth isn't just about financial gain; it's about the cultural and creative impact you leave behind. By scaling sustainably and creating thoughtful, high-value works, you solidify your position not only as a public domain publisher but also as a trailblazer reshaping how these works are perceived and enjoyed. With every book, collection, and partnership, you contribute to a legacy that will inspire and enrich readers for generations to come.

Through collaboration, diversification, and careful planning, you're creating more than a profitable business. You're crafting a future where public domain treasures find new life, reaching audiences in ways never imagined before.

Chapter Ten

Avoiding Pitfalls and Sustaining Profitability

Navigating the world of public domain publishing offers a rare and exciting blend of creative freedom and entrepreneurial opportunity. The vast library of public domain works provides a treasure trove of content that can be transformed, revitalized, and presented to new audiences in innovative ways. But while the potential is immense, this field is not without its challenges. Just like any business venture, success in public domain publishing requires careful planning, strategic decision-making, and a willingness to adapt to an evolving marketplace.

At first glance, it may seem that working with public domain content removes many of the hurdles traditional publishing entails. You bypass the labor-intensive process of original authorship, gain access to materials free of royalty or licensing fees, and tap into literature that has already stood the test of time. However, this ease can be misleading. Without a clear strategy and a thorough understanding of the landscape, publishers can quickly encounter roadblocks, whether it's legal complications due to copyright misunderstandings, stagnant sales from oversaturated markets, or creative burnout from pursuing repetitive ideas.

This chapter focuses on equipping you with the insights and tools needed to avoid those pitfalls and position your projects for long-term success. You'll learn how to steer clear of common mistakes that derail new publishers, like failing to properly verify a work's public domain status or ignoring the need to add unique value to your releases. We'll emphasize the importance of staying up to date on copyright law changes to ensure legal compliance and to capitalize on newly available works as they enter the public domain.

Market research serves as another defining element of a thriving public domain business, and this chapter will show you how to make it an integral part of your strategy. Understanding the needs, desires, and habits of your audience is critical for choosing the right projects and creating content that stands out. Lastly, we'll explore the power of diversification—not only as a way to grow revenue streams but also as a means of keeping your work relevant and creatively fulfilling.

By approaching public domain publishing with a balance of creativity and discipline, you can unlock both financial and personal rewards. This chapter will guide you through the key principles and practices that allow you to build a sustainable and profitable enterprise in this exciting and often overlooked space.

Recognizing and Overcoming Common Mistakes

Every business venture is a learning process, and public domain publishing is no different. The opportunities are vast, but so are the potential pitfalls. Being aware of these challenges and tackling them head-on can make the difference between a thriving enterprise and a frustrating experience. By addressing common mistakes early and employing thoughtful strategies, you're setting yourself on a path to long-term success.

The Critical Importance of Verifying Public Domain Status

One of the most fundamental tasks in public domain publishing is ensuring that the content you want to use is genuinely in the public domain. This may sound straightforward, but it's a step that can result in significant consequences if overlooked. Copyright laws are intricate, and even one small mistake in understanding these laws can lead to costly legal disputes, copyright infringement claims, and unnecessary stress.

For instance, not all works published before a certain date are automatically public domain. Variations in regional copyright laws, extensions introduced for specific kinds of content, or works that were once public domain but later reinstated under exclusive arrangements all add to the complexity of determining a text's status. That's why due diligence is non-negotiable. Tools such as Project Gutenberg, Google Books, and government copyright databases can serve as your first line of defense in verifying the status of a work. Using a combination of these resources and consulting copyright specialists or legal experts when in doubt can help you avoid common mishaps. When it comes to public domain verification, it's far better to invest extra time than to gamble with potential legal repercussions.

Enhancing Public Domain Content for Today's Readers

Another major stumbling block for new publishers is overlooking the need to enhance or reinvent public domain material. Simply reissuing a book as it was originally written might seem like the quickest way to market, but it's rarely the most effective. The expectations of modern audiences have changed, and they demand more than just a faithful reproduction of past works.

Take a moment to think about the original work's language, cultural relevance, and accessibility. Is the prose outdated? Are the themes no longer intuitive for today's readers? Could the material be presented in a way that makes it easier to consume or more visually appealing? Making intentional updates, such as modernizing language or incorporating additional context and commentary, helps set your version apart. Adding high-quality illustrations for children's literature or creating thoughtful annotations for literary classics can breathe new life into old works. The goal isn't to erase the original essence but to amplify it in ways that resonate with today's audience.

Presentation matters just as much as content. Readers are drawn to polished, professional designs that convey attention to detail. From formatting a print layout to designing an eye-catching cover, each small improvement makes an outsized difference in how your product is perceived. Ultimately, people remember experiences, and enhancing both the content and the presentation creates a product that goes beyond being just another reprint.

Steering Away from Oversaturated Markets

The allure of popular genres and trending topics is hard to resist, but following the crowd can lead you to an overpopulated and highly competitive space. The same way countless authors are drawn to widely known niches like romance or self-help, public domain publishers often gravitate toward famous classics or frequently used collections. This can lead to a scenario where your project struggles for visibility, buried among dozens, or even hundreds, of similar offerings.

To avoid this dilemma, it's necessary to dig deeper and identify under-represented niches. Ask yourself what audiences are yearning for but struggling to find. Niche content like historical training manuals, unique folktales, or overlooked poetry collections may not immediately seem like big sellers, but in a focused market with little competition, these projects can grab attention. Sometimes, it pays to think creatively about crossovers between niches, like merging classic literature with contemporary guided journals or forming bilingual editions of foreign language masterpieces that cater to language learners.

Uncovering these opportunities requires targeted market research. Spending time analyzing reviews, speaking with readers, or using tools like Google Trends reveals where unmet demand exists. By entering these less-crowded spaces, you not only improve your chances of standing out but also create a reputation for catering to overlooked or underserved audiences.

Building Resilience Through Awareness

Mistakes are unavoidable in any venture, but understanding the common pitfalls of public domain publishing allows you to approach your work with foresight. Verifying a work's status isn't just a technical step; it sets the foundation for everything that follows. Enhancing content and presentation isn't a chore; it's an opportunity to connect with readers in meaningful ways. Approaching market choices strategically isn't about playing it safe; it's about positioning yourself where success is ripe for the taking. Combining these elements strengthens your position as a publisher who not only survives but thrives in the world of public domain.

Staying Ahead of Copyright Law Changes

Copyright laws are not static; they shift and change over time as governments, organizations, and societies respond to new technologies and evolving perspectives on intellectual property. For those working in public domain publishing, these changes can feel like both a moving target and a treasure map. Staying current on copyright developments is more than a mere formality; it's an essential part of protecting your business and seizing new opportunities as they arise.

Adapting to the Evolution of Copyright Terms

One of the most impactful ways copyright laws continue to evolve is through the extension of copyright terms. These changes have far-reaching implications on when specific works become available in the public domain. For example, in the United States, the Copyright Term Extension Act (sometimes called the "Mickey Mouse Protection Act") delayed the entry of many works into the public domain by an additional 20 years. While such changes can be frustrating for publishers eager to access new material, they underscore the importance of being well-informed about key dates and legislative updates.

Understanding regional differences is just as critical. Different countries follow specific timelines and rules for copyright expiration, which means a book that is public domain in one part of the world may still be under protection in another. For instance, the copyright rules in the European Union often differ significantly from those in the United States, even for works by the same author. Publishers who fail to recognize these nuances risk inadvertently violating copyright law, which can lead to financial losses and legal action.

Keeping track of these developments allows you to prepare for the predictable cycles of new public domain releases. Often, the start of a new year marks the moment when a notable wave of works becomes free to republish. Planning your projects to coincide with these waves can give you a competitive head start, allowing you to release freshly available content while the market is still uncrowded. Being among the first publishers to reintroduce a newly available work not only attracts early interest but also positions you as a forward-thinking leader in your niche.

The Practical Strategies for Staying Updated

Staying informed about changes in copyright law might seem daunting, but it's entirely manageable with the right approach. Begin by integrating credible sources of legal and industry updates into your routines. Subscribing to newsletters from authoritative groups, such as copyright offices or intellectual property law firms, is an easy way to receive timely and relevant information. Many of these organizations offer plain-language summaries of legal updates, saving you the effort of parsing dense legal jargon.

Professional forums, online communities, and industry groups also provide valuable insight. Joining these networks enables you to connect with others in public domain publishing who share similar concerns and goals. Many groups discuss how new copyright rulings or legislative changes affect their projects. Being an active participant not only keeps you informed but also helps you build a network of peers you can rely on for advice.

Educational courses, webinars, and workshops focused on copyright law are additional resources worth considering. While some may have a cost, the knowledge you gain can prevent expensive legal mistakes in the future. Tech-savvy publishers can also set keyword alerts for topics like "copyright law changes" or "new public domain works" to automatically capture the latest updates from news sources, blogs, and academic articles.

The Legal and Creative Advantages of Preparedness

Remaining compliant with copyright laws is more than just a safeguard against potential legal issues; it's a strategic advantage that allows you to act decisively when opportunities emerge. When you know which works are entering the public domain and plan accordingly, you can seize the moment to roll out well-prepared, high-quality editions ahead of the competition.

For instance, consider the wave of works entering the U.S. public domain each January due to copyright protection lapsing 95 years after publication. By understanding this timeline, a publisher can prepare by choosing a work in advance, designing enhancements to make it stand out, and timing a release for maximum impact. Competitors who aren't as vigilant may not realize these works are available until it's too late.

There's also a creative element to being informed. Knowing about upcoming releases allows you to identify promising opportunities while remaining legally sound. A strong grasp of copyright timelines enables you to plan longer-term projects, such as launching a thematic series or developing supplementary materials like companion guides, audiobooks, or educational resources.

Strengthening Your Foundation Through Knowledge

Navigating the complexities of copyright law can feel like exploring a labyrinth, but the rewards for diligence and foresight are far-reaching. Staying ahead of copyright law changes not only shields your business from costly errors but also empowers you to act swiftly and confidently on emerging opportunities. It's an investment in knowledge that can transform your public domain publishing endeavors from reactive to highly strategic.

By committing to continual learning and employing accessible resources to track developments, you're building a business foundation that isn't just legally solid – it's primed for growth. With laws already in motion and new opportunities on the horizon, staying informed ensures that your creative and entrepreneurial aspirations align seamlessly with the evolving rules of public domain publishing.

The Power of Ongoing Market Research

The tastes and interests of readers are constantly evolving, and what captured attention yesterday may no longer be relevant tomorrow. Understanding your audience is not a luxury; it's a necessity for anyone looking to sustain profitability in public domain publishing. Unlike a static project that you complete and walk away from, the publishing business requires you to keep your finger on the pulse of shifting trends and preferences. Market research isn't a one-time task. It's a continuous process that keeps you agile, ensuring you can adapt to your audience's changing demands and emerging opportunities.

Keeping Up with Trends and Opportunities

To stay ahead in the crowded marketplace of public domain content, it's crucial to identify and tap into emerging trends before they become oversaturated. Tools like Google Trends can provide insights into what people are searching for and how their interests are changing over time. Similarly, social media platforms, including Twitter, Instagram, TikTok, and Pinterest, offer a wealth of data on current conversations, trending hashtags, and themes that resonate with different demographics.

For example, suppose interest in a beloved classic author like Jane Austen resurges, fueled by a hit adaptation or viral post. You could capitalize on this wave by offering enhanced versions of her works with modern commentary, unique illustrations, or bundled collections. The key is to be proactive. By monitoring these signals, you position yourself to respond quickly and effectively, releasing content when demand is at its peak.

Platforms like Amazon can also provide invaluable insights. By studying customer reviews and examining "Customers Also Bought" sections for similar public domain works, you can uncover what readers feel is missing or what they're craving more of. Paying attention to genres or themes that see steady growth, such as mindfulness or sustainability, helps you align your offerings with cultural momentum.

Listening to Your Audience

While external tools and platforms offer broad insights, nothing is more valuable than hearing directly from your own readers. Building a system to capture and analyze customer feedback can transform how you approach future projects. Encourage readers to leave reviews on your books or share thoughts via your website or social media channels. Craft open-ended questions that invite deeper responses, such as what they enjoyed most, what could have been done better, or what they'd love to see next.

Surveys are another effective method to gather targeted input. Sending brief questionnaires to your email subscribers or social media followers allows you to fine-tune your offerings based on their preferences. For instance, if you're considering republishing a collection of forgotten fairy tales, you could ask your audience whether they prefer annotated editions or creative illustrations, ensuring your next project aligns with what they're excited to buy.

The benefits don't stop there. Seeking feedback not only helps you sharpen your strategy but also forges a stronger relationship with your readers. When customers see that you value their input, they feel a sense of connection and loyalty to your brand. This connection translates into repeat sales, positive word-of-mouth referrals, and a community of devoted readers who support your work over the long term.

Innovating Through Insight

Market research also fuels innovation, helping you identify untapped potential in the public domain. What sets you apart in a crowded marketplace isn't just your ability to reproduce existing works but your vision to breathe new life into them. For example, you might discover a growing interest in foreign language content and decide to create bilingual editions of public domain classics, catering to language learners. Alternatively, you might identify a trend in minimalist design and create a line of visually striking, simplified editions that appeal to modern aesthetic sensibilities.

Don't limit yourself to the book world when exploring inspiration. Trends in adjacent industries, such as entertainment, gaming, or education, can spark fresh ideas for how to present or market your content. For instance, a popular historical drama series might inspire you to repackage period-specific public domain works or curate thematic collections related to the time period of the show. By researching where culture is heading, you give yourself the tools to adapt creatively and remain relevant.

Building a Feedback-Driven Ecosystem

The most successful public domain publishers don't just react to trends; they create ecosystems where feedback continually informs decision-making. By fostering an ongoing dialogue between you and your readers, you build a business that moves in tandem with their needs and expectations. This iterative process allows each project to be more refined than the last, cultivating a library of works that feel deeply relevant and thoughtfully crafted.

Ultimately, ongoing market research isn't just about following trends or satisfying curiosity. It's about staying connected to the people who matter most in your business. Their changing preferences and untapped desires aren't obstacles; they're opportunities. By leaning into this evolving relationship, you lay the foundation for a publishing enterprise that isn't just profitable but enduring, vibrant, and endlessly innovative.

Diversifying Creative Projects to Maintain Relevance

Remaining relevant in a competitive and ever-changing market requires more than simply finding a winning formula and sticking to it. Diversification isn't just a survival strategy; it's a way to unlock new opportunities, spark creative energy, and build a resilient business that can weather fluctuations in demand. When you explore new formats, genres, and approaches, you not only expand your reach but also future-proof your work against the natural ebbs and flows of audience tastes. Diversification ensures that your creative endeavors remain vibrant and rewarding, both financially and personally.

Exploring New Formats within Your Existing Projects

One of the easiest ways to begin diversifying is by reimagining your existing content in fresh formats. Public domain works lend themselves beautifully to repurposing because they aren't reliant on one single presentation. If you've published an eBook of a classic novel, think about how you can bring that same material to life in other ways. For instance, audiobooks are becoming increasingly popular, especially as more people turn to convenient, on-the-go methods of consuming content. Recording a high-quality audiobook version allows you to tap into a growing market of listeners who crave literary classics but may not have time to read.

Print editions are another valuable option. While digital formats are easy to distribute and market, there remains a strong audience for physical books. By offering print-on-demand versions, you provide readers with something tangible and create an opportunity to add unique design elements, such as custom covers or illustrations, that make your edition stand out. People love the tactile experience of turning pages, and beautifully designed physical copies can often command premium prices.

You can also expand your releases by creating supplementary materials. A public domain text can act as the foundation for workbooks, study guides, or companion materials. Imagine pairing a literary classic with an interactive journal designed to explore the text's themes or a modern guide to interpreting its symbolism. Such add-ons create new revenue streams while giving readers a deeper, more engaging experience.

Venturing Into New Genres and Topics

Diversification isn't limited to repackaging your current projects. Experimenting with entirely different genres or subjects can open doors to untapped markets and help you reach new audiences. For example, if your current focus has been on republishing literary classics, why not explore the world of historical nonfiction? You could adapt original historical texts into digestible formats for use in classrooms or by amateur historians. Maps, timelines, and commentary woven into the original narratives not only add educational value but also transform serious materials into approachable, engaging resources.

Children's literature, particularly fairy tales and fables from the public domain, offers another fertile ground for diversification. A collection of old tales can inspire illustrations, storytelling animations, and educational children's books that captivate younger audiences. Taking the stories a step further, you could develop coloring books, activity books, or even animated storytime videos. The possibilities are endless when you consider how public domain works can be modernized to fit various age groups and consumption preferences.

Thinking creatively about hybrid concepts is another exciting avenue. Merging genres or mediums into something entirely new can set you apart from traditional publishers. For instance, you might reimagine a selection of classic poetry as mindfulness prompts, pairing individual pieces with calming designs and guided exercises. Or you could mix historical texts with a fictional narrative, creating an entirely new type of storytelling that introduces younger readers to real-world events through an engaging, fictionalized lens. By thinking outside the box, you create products that are not only unique but also deeply impactful for niche audiences.

Beautifying Business Sustainability with Variety

Diversification offers more than just financial rewards; it adds a layer of depth and excitement to your daily work. Running busy, high-output creative projects can be exhausting, and the risk of burnout is very real. When you're caught in the rhythm of churning out similar types of content over and over, the creative spark that drew you to this work in the first place can begin to fade. Experimenting with varied formats, genres, and audiences can reinvigorate your sense of purpose and make your entire process feel fresh.

Constantly challenging yourself to try something new encourages personal growth and keeps your entrepreneurial spirit alive. This doesn't mean abandoning your core focus, but rather enhancing it by exploring spaces you hadn't yet considered. Tackling children's projects, attempting new visual design techniques, or creating multimedia components will introduce you to new skills and collaborators that inspire deeper engagement with your work. The energy you bring back to your creative ventures will translate directly to the quality of your output, making it more compelling for your audience.

Building a Portfolio That Stands the Test of Time

A diversified creative portfolio has the ability to weather change in ways a single-stream approach cannot. If one project underperforms or a particular medium falls out of favor, you have other ventures to lean on while rethinking what comes next. This doesn't just safeguard your profit; it creates a dynamic model of creativity that can pivot and grow as trends transform and markets fluctuate.

By diversifying your public domain publishing projects, you're not only protecting your business from temporary challenges but also opening up a world of new opportunities. From audiobooks to children's animation, from workbook supplements to entirely new genres, the spectrum of possibilities is as large as your imagination. This approach ensures that your work remains relevant, impactful, and, above all, creatively fulfilling. Ultimately, by broadening your focus, you're crafting a publishing legacy that is not only profitable but endlessly adaptable and inspiring.

Building a Business That Endures

Creating a lasting business in public domain publishing goes far beyond chasing the next trendy release or racing to flood the market with quick, low-effort offerings. True sustainability requires strategy, care, and a vision for the future. It's about transforming the wealth of public domain literature into something meaningful, relevant, and valuable for modern audiences. This approach not only sustains profitability but also builds a foundation for long-term success.

One of the cornerstones of an enduring business is avoiding the costly mistakes that can derail your efforts. By taking the time to verify the copyright status of the works you use, staying compliant with evolving laws, and prioritizing quality over speed, you protect your reputation and avoid unnecessary setbacks. A stable business is built on a commitment to detail, and that commitment ensures that your efforts are both legally sound and creatively impactful.

Staying informed about copyright developments is equally critical. Changes in legislation can shape the future of your publishing potential, and those who anticipate these shifts are better positioned to seize opportunities. Being proactive rather than reactive allows you to stay ahead of the curve, ensuring your business is never caught off-guard and that you maximize the release of newly available works.

Market research plays another vital role in longevity. The needs and desires of your audience will inevitably evolve, and maintaining an ongoing connection with those trends ensures you'll remain relevant. By listening to your readers and analyzing the marketplace, you can adapt and innovate. A business that listens is never stagnant; it grows and evolves alongside its audience, deepening its impact year after year.

Diversification is the final piece of the puzzle, offering not only financial stability but creative fulfillment. Expanding into new formats and ideas provides a buffer against unforeseen challenges while keeping your work fresh and engaging. Whether it's through audiobooks, children's adaptations, or educational resources, exploring different paths can keep your business dynamic and resilient. Diversification ensures that your work remains exciting for both you and your readers, helping you avoid burnout while enriching your publishing catalog.

Yet, beyond these individual practices lies the true secret to building a business that lasts: a genuine passion for what you do. Public domain publishing is more than an entrepreneurial endeavor; it's a creative mission powered by the opportunity to breathe new life into timeless works. When you lead with care and creativity, you produce more than profit. You create a legacy of literature that inspires, educates, and entertains across generations.

Sustained success in public domain publishing isn't about luck. It's about combining sharp strategy with unwavering consistency and an enduring love for the craft. This thoughtful, balanced approach not only builds a business capable of withstanding market shifts but also elevates the cultural significance of the works you share. By mastering the principles of avoiding mistakes, staying informed, researching with intent, and diversifying boldly, you arm yourself with the tools to create something far greater than a business. You create a bridge between the past and the present, revitalizing forgotten gems of literature for the audiences of today and tomorrow.

Your dedication to this process ensures that your efforts will stand the test of time, leaving behind more than a profitable venture. You're building an enduring impact in the literary landscape, offering new life to works that might otherwise have been forgotten while enriching the world with the treasures of the past.

Resources Appendix

This appendix offers a comprehensive list of tools, websites, and platforms to support your success in public domain publishing. These resources are carefully curated to help you verify copyright status, conduct market research, create and distribute your content, and stay informed about the latest developments in copyright law.

Verifying Copyright Status

Ensuring the works you plan to use have truly entered the public domain is essential to operating a legally compliant and trustworthy publishing venture. The following resources can help you accurately verify copyright status:

- **Project Gutenberg**

  A vast library of public domain texts that have been carefully screened for copyright compliance. Ideal for sourcing high-quality, freely available literature.

  Website: www.gutenberg.org

- **HathiTrust Digital Library**
  An invaluable resource for accessing a wide variety of digitized books and other materials, many of which are in the public domain.
  Website: www.hathitrust.org

- **Stanford Copyright Renewal Database**
  This database allows you to confirm whether a U.S. copyright was renewed, giving you clarity about works published between 1923 and 1963.
  Website: renewals.copyright.gov

- **U.S. Copyright Office Public Catalog**
  Contains registration and renewal records for works copyrighted from 1978 to the present, as well as some earlier works. A key tool for confirming copyright status.
  Website: publicrecords.copyright.gov

- **Google Books**
  Use Google Books to check if a work is labeled as public domain, especially for older texts that may require additional verification.
  Website: books.google.com

Staying Informed About Copyright Law

Copyright laws are dynamic and vary by region. Use these resources to stay updated on changes in legislation and their potential impact on public domain publishing:

- **World Intellectual Property Organization (WIPO)**

Provides authoritative information about global copyright laws and treaties, allowing you to stay informed about international developments.
Website: www.wipo.int

- **Creative Commons**
  Though best known for modern licensing, Creative Commons offers resources to understand the boundaries of copyright and the public domain.
  Website: creativecommons.org

- **Copyright Alliance**
  A useful hub for learning about copyright legislation, interpretations, and trends impacting creators and publishers. Subscribe to their updates to stay ahead.
  Website: copyrightalliance.org

- **University of Pennsylvania Online Books Page**
  Offers detailed public domain resources as well as educational information on copyright timelines and laws.
  Website: onlinebooks.library.upenn.edu

Conducting Market Research

Successful public domain publishing requires a deep understanding of your audience and market trends. The following platforms help you gather data and insights to inform your decisions:

- **Google Trends**
  Analyze search trends and audience interest over time to identify profitable niches and time your releases strategical-

ly.
Website: trends.google.com

- **Amazon Bestsellers and Reviews**
  Study the bestseller lists to identify high-performing categories and examine customer reviews for insights into what
  readers love or dislike.
  Website: www.amazon.com/best-sellers

- **Social Media Analytics Tools**
  Platforms like Facebook Insights, Pinterest Trends, and Instagram Analytics help you understand modern interests
  and how to connect with target demographics.

- **Goodreads**
  Use Goodreads to find reader reviews, ratings, and discussions centered on popular books, which can provide guidance for improving your editions or exploring untapped
  niches.
  Website: www.goodreads.com

- **Niche-Specific Online Communities**
  Forums like Reddit (e.g., r/books, r/selfpublish) or specialized Facebook groups can provide authentic insights from
  avid readers, writers, and publishers.

Creating and Distributing Content

Public domain works often require thoughtful enhancements and
careful distribution to stand out. These tools help you update, publish, and market your projects effectively:

- **Canva**

  A user-friendly design platform for creating eye-catching book covers, marketing visuals, and supplementary materials.

  Website: www.canva.com

- **Scrivener**

  An excellent tool for writing, organizing, and editing long-form content like annotated editions or compilations of public domain works.

  Website: www.literatureandlatte.com/scrivener/overview

- **Audacity**

  A free, open-source audio editing tool perfect for creating high-quality audiobooks.

  Website: www.audacityteam.org

- **KDP (Kindle Direct Publishing)**

  Amazon's self-publishing platform allows you to release both eBooks and print-on-demand paperbacks, giving you global access to millions of readers.

  Website: kdp.amazon.com

- **ACX (Audiobook Creation Exchange)**

  ACX connects you with narrators to produce audiobooks for distribution on platforms like Audible and iTunes.

  Website: www.acx.com

- **Draft2Digital**

  Simplifies the process of distributing both eBooks and print editions across multiple platforms like Apple Books, Barnes & Noble, and Kobo.

Website: www.draft2digital.com

- **Etsy**

  For handcrafted or niche items like beautifully designed print editions or supplemental materials, Etsy provides a unique platform for reaching targeted buyers.
  Website: www.etsy.com

- **Grammarly**

  Enhance the quality of your written content with this AI-based proofreading and grammar-checking tool.
  Website: www.grammarly.com

Inspirational Archives and Rare Finds

Sometimes, the hardest part is discovering unique or underutilized materials. These archives and libraries are ideal for uncovering hidden gems that might captivate modern audiences:

- **Internet Archive**

  A massive collection of texts, audio, and video, much of which is in the public domain. A great resource for finding overlooked works.
  Website: archive.org

- **Digital Public Library of America (DPLA)**

  Access millions of items—including books, journals, and images—from libraries, archives, and museums across the U.S.
  Website: dp.la

- **Europeana Collections**

Explore Europe's digital platform for cultural heritage, featuring a wealth of public domain material perfect for international audiences.
Website: www.europeana.eu

- **Library of Congress Digital Collections**
A treasure trove of American history and culture, offering public domain texts, photographs, and more.
Website: www.loc.gov/collections

Leveraging these resources will empower you to verify copyright status, identify market trends, produce high-quality content, and distribute it effectively. Public domain publishing is a craft that blends strategic thinking with creativity, and these tools are here to support your efforts every step of the way. With the right resources and a commitment to excellence, you can transform timeless works into extraordinary opportunities.

About the Author

Gerry Marrs, Ph.D. is an American author, entrepreneur, and former U.S. Air Force veteran widely recognized for his practical, results-driven guides on personal finance, entrepreneurship, and self-improvement. Following a distinguished 21-year military career specializing in manpower and personnel management, Dr. Marrs transitioned into writing, leveraging his extensive experience in business administration and organizational development. He is dedicated to helping readers navigate financial challenges, achieve economic independence, and build sustainable income streams.

Notable Books by Gerry Marrs:

- "Free Money For Nearly Anything"

- "How to Make Money Writing Product Reviews"

- "How to Legally Rob Credit-Card Companies"

- "60 Days to $60,000"

- "The Hidden Money Manual"

- "How to Make $800 Per Month Starting Tonight!"

- "Stop Writing New Books!"

- "From Zero to Meme Coin Hero"

Where to Buy His Books:
- Amazon: https://www.amazon.com/stores/author/B00GVJ4N0C

- Everand (formerly Scribd): https://www.everand.com/author/729208167/Gerry-Marrs

- Bookshop.org: https://bookshop.org/contributors/gerry-marrs

- Waterstones: https://www.waterstones.com/author/gerry-marrs/6949694

- Audible: https://www.audible.com/author/Gerry-Marrs/B00GVJ4N0C

- Storytel: https://www.storytel.com/sg/publishers/gerry-marrs-publications-65532

Connect with Gerry Marrs:
- Facebook: https://www.facebook.com/GerryMarrs/

- Official   Website: https://www.gerrymarrspublications.com/

Whether you're aiming to improve your financial health, explore new sources of income, or start your self-publishing journey, Dr. Marrs provides valuable insights and actionable strategies to guide you toward success.

www.ingramcontent.com/pod-product-compliance
Lightning Source LLC
Chambersburg PA
CBHW070928260726
48661CB00003B/878